Extreme Personality Makeover

Dr. Mels Carbonell

Uniquely You™ Resources

Extreme Personality Makeover
Published by Uniquely You™ Resources

Copyright © 2005 by Mels Carbonell

Uniquely You™ is a trademark of Uniquely You, Inc.
and is registered in the
U.S. Patent and Trademark Office.
Printed in the United States of America

ALL RIGHTS RESERVED
No part of this publication may be reproduced,
stored in a retrieval system, or transmitted,
in any form or by any means —
electronic, mechanical, photocopying,
recording, or otherwise —
without prior written permission.

For more information:
Uniquely You™ Resources
Post Office Box 490
Blue Ridge, GA 30513

Phone: (706) 492-5490
Email: drmels@myuy.com

ISBN: 1-888846-03-8

TABLE OF CONTENTS

Introduction 6

Chapter One 13
    Make the decision to have a makeover!

Chapter Two 23
    Accept the "way" God made your personality!

Chapter Three 35
    Know your strengths and "uniquenesses!"

Chapter Four 55
    Emulate the good traits of all the personality types!

Chapter Five 73
    Overcome your doubts and obstacles!

Chapter Six 83
    Visualize what you can become!

Chapter Seven 95
    Exercise each personality type to improve them!

Chapter Eight 105
    Renew your commitment daily!

Postscript 117

To all my friends, over the past nearly 40 years of ministry, who have loved me and tolerated my personality, I dedicate this book. There are too many acquaintances to mention and so many friends I could name, plus a few dear friends to share my appreciation for allowing me to be and then become what God has wanted for my personality and life.

Without their friendship and patience with me, I probably would have never survived the road blocks and pot holes of life, especially in my ministry.

Above all, I want to thank the Lord Jesus Christ for His enduring love and workmanship in my life. Having gone through all I have experienced, especially early in my life, and to now enjoy His abundant blessings, I am eternally grateful.

Mels Carbonell, Ph.D.

PREFACE

Dear Reader,

The bottom line of this book is to influence everyone who has the attitude of "that's just the way I am" and to help those who simply desire to improve themselves for God's glory. My goal is to help you develop a renewed personality in Christ. Most people like or dislike their personalities. I am not saying there is anything wrong with your personality to feel either way about it. The issue is not changing your personality, it is controlling its power over you that really matters.

The practical application is to understand how to adapt our personalities to the needs of others, rather than expecting everyone to blindly accept our personalities in spite of our strengths and "uniqueness."

Once we comprehend the will and way of God working through our personalities, we can then become the person He wants us to be. We can then conform our personalities into the image of Christ and reflect His life in us.

We should seek to be like Him and not demand that people accept our bad personality traits. God is not finished with us, and this book is an instructional manual showing how to remodel and renew our lives through an Extreme Personality Makeover.

Thank you for allowing me to serve you!

Mels Carbonell, Ph.D.

Introduction

What did you think when you first heard or read the title: "Extreme Personality Makeover!" Did you wonder, "What does that mean?" or "Sounds interesting!" Or perhaps you did not know what to think!

It seems that people are having expensive beauty treatments, reconstructive surgeries or home makeovers in record numbers today. It is a nationwide trend that seems to indicate something significant about why we do what we do.

We have gone from simply remodeling homes or having minor surgeries, to major overhauls of ourselves and our homes. We have gone from makeovers to now having "extreme" makeovers. What is it about our society that we are not satisfied with a simple fix-it? Why do we now insist on monumental measures?

Extreme makeovers have become an obsession, as well as fascinating human interest stories. What if you could have an extreme *personality* makeover? Would you like to have a winning personality — a personality that everyone relates to?

How about having a personality that can respond best in every difficult situation? Even if you already have a pleasing personality, would you like to improve it and make it even better? An "extreme personality makeover" may be just what you need and / or want.

First of all, I must stress I am not saying there is anything wrong with your personality that requires changing. No one has a "bad" personality. It is what you *do* with your personality that is good or bad.

We can all improve our strengths and avoid our "uniqueness." We can also learn from the personalities of others to increase our effectiveness. A personality makeover will not hurt us and it may even help, especially with our relationships and ministries.

The word, "extreme" may seem radical to some people, but it may be just what they have been searching for. Others may require minor adjustments rather than major overhauls. Regardless, we can all benefit from the understanding of how our personalities must become more flexible. It can especially help us improve our task and / or people skills!

It is really all about controlling, not changing, our personalities!

Unfortunately, it may seem very self-centered, but it is not. We should first recognize how God made us perfect, but we chose to determine our own destinies and rebel against Him. When humankind turned its back on God, our personalities began to be infected with all the little twists that cause the problems we have with people.

Christ, the greatest teacher, is seen in the Holy Scriptures standing at the door of our lives inviting us to learn from Him. He wants to show us the way to forgiveness and happiness. He desires to enter our lives and become our Savior and Counselor.

We were originally created with personalities, but we went astray. Our once perfect personalities have since developed weaknesses and "uniqueness" that clash with other personality types. God never intended us to conflict with others. He desired harmony and happiness in our lives.

This may seem like an unusual concept. It is actually a spiritual approach to a psychological or personal problem everyone has — getting along with others. This understanding developed from my years as a "Human Behavior Consultant" and seeing how people have been impacted by adapting their personalities to "become all things to all people."

My concern is for those people who have the attitude — "That's just the way I am!" They do not want a makeover, or even think they need one. They limit the divine power of God to "finish" His work in their lives. They have not understood the reality of how God wants to control their personalities so all the good traits are evident in their lives. It is a human drama played out in their everyday experiences and it clamors for a solution.

Television Drama

Today's "reality shows" are on the rise because people enjoy seeing changes from one extreme to the other. They dream of the day when they could have their makeover. The reality is we are actually where we are right now, because that is what we have chosen. We may often dream about having a more effective personality. A makeover could be our dream come true.

Having an extreme personality makeover can change your life. It can help you relate and work with people on a higher plane. You do not have to be limited by your personality's shortcomings or weaknesses ("uniqueness"). You can be liberated to be free of your limitations. You can experience freedom to be more than just being yourself.

You can become anyone you want to. If you are quiet and shy, you can learn how to be expressive and influencing. If you are dominant to a fault, you can learn to be so kind that people enjoy you, rather than endure you.

This is not about manipulation! It is more about understanding the Holy Scriptures and the "Science of Human Behavior." It is about why people do what they do. It is about learning from others so you can be what they need you to be. It is not about being unnatural, but rather, being supernatural. It is about learning the biblical principles that will allow you to be what God has designed you to be, with all the good traits and none of the bad traits.

If you act in ways that seem irritating or ineffective with others, then you are a perfect candidate for an extreme personality makeover. If you desire to be more than what you are on the surface, then get ready for new and revolutionary insights that will impact your life!

Some people may think this is ridiculous!

They immediately conclude it is nothing but an attempt to boost our self-worth or image. However, it is not an ego trip. It is very serious, because it relates to how we see ourselves and how people see God in us. It is paramount, because it represents who and Whose we are. What people see in us is how our lives count in this seemingly purposeless existence.

We want others to think of more than our images; we want them to see a reflection of God "working in us both to will and do of His good pleasure" (Phil. 2:13). Having an extreme personality makeover is actually letting God make us over so that we reflect and shine for Him.

Being "conformed to the image of God" (Rom. 8:29) will be an extraordinary experience for most people. It begins with understanding how He wants to be more than just an invited "guest" in our lives. He wants to be the "Head" of our lives. He wants to make us over from our feet to our face, from our attitudes to our actions.

It all begins with the recognition that we need a power greater than ourselves if we are going to be better than what we have made of ourselves. This means we must humble ourselves and recognize we are incomplete without God. His divine makeover begins with you coming to Him by grace through faith alone (Eph. 2:8,9).

Many people call this a "salvation experience." Others refer to it as being "born again." More people recognize it as having a "personal relationship with God." Regardless of how it is referred to, no one can really know God without coming to Him by faith. Scripture teaches, "Without faith it is impossible to please God" (Heb. 11:6). It is absolutely essential before we can experience our divine makeover.

Once we acknowledge our need of a Savior from ourselves and the error of our ways (sin), we are ready to understand how God can give us new life and direction. We cannot have a makeover until we recognize that the work we have done with ourselves is insufficient. Otherwise, we would not need an extreme makeover.

Some people will stop here and think: "I don't think I need a makeover. I'm okay just the way I am. I don't want anyone telling me to trust in anyone other than myself!" That is a sure indication that those people definitely need an "extreme" encounter with the One Who originally made them.

God made us pure and perfect.

He also gave us the will to choose our own path in life. Any direction apart from His way is the wrong way. It leads to frustration and failure. God's way leads to forgiveness, peace, and assurance.

The question now is, do you really think you can handle the trials and troubles of life better than God can? Do you actually feel He knows what is best for you? Your makeover must begin with the reality that you need Him to solve the difficult challenges of life and to make you all you can be.

Introduction

Once you decide to let Him be your Savior and extreme life-planner, you can experience a makeover for the rest of your life here on earth and for all eternity. Acknowledge your need for Him and trust in the finished work of Christ on the cross. Jesus did what you could not do for yourself: He lived a perfect life. He paid the sin-debt on Calvary's cross necessary for your forgiveness. He also wants to give you a spiritual makeover while you live, as well as eternal life when you die.

Your self-dependence to get to heaven by your good works has separated you from God. That self-sufficiency has to be reconciled with Him in order to have a relationship with God. His makeover begins with you coming to Him in childlike faith.

What He did on the cross was the payment you could never afford to pay. He literally gave His life for you to have His life. He bore your blame. He suffered your shame — all because He loved you (John 3:16) and wanted to have a personal relationship with you (John 10:10). He literally paid for everything you have ever done wrong. All you can do is to totally believe He died and rose again for you to be forgiven and personally know Him. This is the gospel truth, the good news that sets people free! (John 8:32)

This is not about having a religious experience.

Religions are man-made. True Christianity is God coming to earth in the person of Jesus Christ, living a sinless life, and dying on the cross to become your Savior. But you must trust Him alone, and biblically and personally believe in Him. It is not believing in Him intellectually. Christ died, that is history, but Christ died for me, that is salvation.

If you have trusted Christ as your Savior, God desires for you to let Him live His life in you and to conform you into the image of His dear Son. If you have not come to faith in Christ, you now have the opportunity to settle it once and for all. Simply take God at His Word and "believe on the Lord Jesus Christ" (Acts 16:31).

On the authority of God's Word (1 John 5:13), you can know — not hope, guess, or wish you have eternal life. Then you are ready to have a divine and extreme personality makeover. The most exciting thing about all this is God will do the makeover in you. It is actually something He will do, if you just learn the principles and truths that will set you free. He wants to live His life in and through you (Gal 2:20).

He will do all the work if you will just do all the trusting and obeying (1 Thess. 5:24). There is no better way to be happy in Jesus and throughout your everyday life than to "just trust and obey." He will not only save your soul from eternal separation from God, but He will also save you from yourself here on earth. He will make you over to become the person He intended you to be. You can have an extreme personality makeover for His glory and your good!

*M*ake The Decision To Have A Makeover!

Everyone needs a personality makeover! Without it we can fall into the trap of just being "ourselves" throughout life. You may wonder, "What's wrong with that?" Nothing, if you are content with a status quo existence and a life that will be stagnant as long as you live.

Actually, that is impossible. Nothing stands still. Nothing, other than Christ, stays the same. We either improve or degenerate! The Second Law of Thermodynamics has discovered that energy always runs down when left alone.

If you do not improve your personality and just leave it alone, it will settle into a powerless, downhill drain in your life. God never intended your personality to become wasted and inefficient. He wants to bless and use your personality to its fullest capability.

You may have heard the saying, "Use it or lose it!"

This thought implies to "improve your personality or lose its potential to bless you and others!" God gave you a specific personality type to make you special. Your personality is just what others lack, and possibly what YOU need to relate better with them.

The personalities of others, as they relate to you, is exactly what you subconsciously yearn for to enjoy life as God intended.

It goes both ways. Your personality is for your benefit and for the blessings of others. Everyone needs a personality makeover to improve how they tend to think, feel, and act throughout their entire lives.

Now, what exactly is an extreme personality makeover? It is extreme because it may be something you never imagined. For some people a makeover may even seem impossible, but with God all things are possible (Mark 10:27). It is also unique and useful, plus it is powerful and practical.

It is extreme because it goes from the absurd to the brilliant. It reaches from one end of our emotions all the way to the other end. It is revolutionary, yet foundational. It can literally transform people's behavior from poor to amazingly profound.

By understanding our drives and identifying our motivations, we can then control them. Without this knowledge we tend to respond to life's challenges according to our instincts and feelings. However, our instincts are often incorrect and our feelings usually fail us.

We must find something better than vague speculations!

We need timeless principles and established truths that do not change from generation to generation. Good directions must come from someone who clearly knows the way.

Extreme thinking in today's post-modern world demands that we return to an unchanging truth that is relative and relational. We can not ask people to have an extreme makeover without explaining how this extreme is better than the alternative.

The post-modern way is to just continue as we have: acting, feeling, and thinking the same way as always. Unfortunately, many people today determine to not get too spiritual or radical.

*M*ake the decision to have a makeover!

The younger generation wants to pick and choose what is best with no strings or pressures attached. Today, teens and young adults want choices, not commitments. They want relationships, not religious platitudes.

Even middle-aged adults are questioning their values and views of what really matters. Everyone seems to be stabbing in the dark at something that is not there. People of all ages are becoming more confused about life and themselves.

Rocky, Sparky, Susie, & Charity

Consider Susie. She is a young single adult looking for more than staying home every weekend and doing nothing. She is so shy she would never think of calling a man and asking him out. She dislikes her personality and would love to have an extreme personality makeover to become more outgoing.

Then there is Sparky, a college student. He is the life of every party. He has tons of friends. He is a social butterfly, but his mouth keeps getting him into trouble. He wishes he could control his reactions and responses. He is too loud and emotional. Some people do not want him around. He is considering taking a class on "improving listening skills." He actually thinks everyone ought to have his type of personality, but recognizes there is room for improvement.

Meet Charity. She is a cautious and conscientious middle-aged mother who worries a lot. She is not sure what her personality is, but is inquiring and researching why many people tend to be so disorganized.

Some people notice her name means "love," but think she lacks warmth because of her obvious judgmental and critical spirit. It does not really bother her, because she is usually right about most things. She is thinking about a personality makeover, but is too indecisive.

And let us not forget Rocky. He is a successful businessman, who tends to be a workaholic. He wants to improve his relationships with others, but is too busy to really work at it. He tends to be impatient and too aggressive. He thinks a personality makeover is ridiculous. He says, "I am what I am and that's all there is to it. If you don't like me, too bad." But he is wrestling with so many broken relationships, he realizes there has to be more than making money. He thinks everyone else should have an extreme personality makeover and become like he is.

Just look at the people around you!

Each of these four types represent the majority of people around you. One of them will probably be somewhat or exactly like you. How should someone appeal to you about having an extreme personality makeover?

It may demand drastic measures. Or it might just require a simple personality makeover. Regardless, everyone should have a diagnosis and prescription to improve their personalities so they will be more educated about their motivations and become more effective with their relationships.

Your personality is the key to unlocking this treasure. Identifying and controlling your personality will make or break the level of your success with people and tasks. You should not ignore it or discard it as unimportant.

You must decide to learn more about your personality. It is the special way you think, feel, and act. It is your divine design that makes you special. It is like a motivational control center in your life. Think of it as just a tool within you, a gauge by which you can read what drives you.

Like any vital organ, our personalities must be nourished and

*M*ake the decision to have a makeover!

grow into healthy parts of our lives. When an organ becomes weak or diseased it can ruin our wellness. We should not ignore it or leave it alone. Our personalities must be fed the Word of God, good thoughts, wise decisions, and healthy feelings. Our personality, much like our organs, must not be left alone to develop whichever way life affects us.

Second Law of Thermodynamics

The Law of Entropy, also known as the Second Law of Thermodynamics, demands that we take care of ourselves. That includes our personalities as well as our bodies. We must exercise our hearts with cardiovascular activities. We should feed our minds positive thoughts. Our blood requires immune-building antioxidants. Physical exercise and proper nutrition grow healthy organs.

Our blood pressure is also very important. Just as we identify our blood type and measure our blood pressure, we should also know our personality type and how to control the pressures of everyday life.

An extreme personality makeover is a little like having a physical exam. Checking your vital signs and having blood work done are essential parts of every exam. Once you have completed the exam, you wait for the results of your blood and EKG tests. Depending on what you discover, you then make the adjustments in your lifestyle to improve your health.

Identifying your personality type is like checking your blood type. No one has a "bad" blood type. Some types are more prevalent than others, but all normal types sustain life. What doctors look for is diseased blood. Knowing the type is not as important as finding disease in the blood.

The same is true with discovering your personality type. The important part of your makeover is not what type of personality you have, but rather how your personality is controlling you or how you are controlling your personality. Once you identify your personality you can begin to learn how your personality is affected by all the elements and influences of life.

Passive People-Oriented Types

For example, if you have a sweet, soft, sensitive, and security-oriented type personality, does it make you so nice that people take advantage of you? Do some people think of you as a "sucker"? Are you vulnerable to codependency, where you become dependent on others to make your decisions for you?

People with these personality types have tremendous traits such as loyalty, kindness, patience, and humility. Under pressure they often become too nice, too kind, and too caring. They are their own worst enemies. Their craving for stability often makes them insecure.

A personality makeover can show them how to control their sensitivity and sweetness so people do not "use" them. They can also learn how to be more aggressive and assertive. Another result from a simple makeover can be improving how to communicate persuasively to large crowds and small groups.

Other personalities will definitely take note of this makeover's different behavior. People will be more responsive. This personality type can go from being a "pushover" or "wimp" to a strong, sharp, and confident person. This person can go from "zero" to "hero" when it comes to looking for someone who can direct, communicate, or evaluate the task at hand.

Their strengths are supporting, listening, and doing what they are told. Their weaknesses ("uniqueness") are the opposites — not initiating, looking the other way, seldom speaking out,

*M*ake the decision to have a makeover!

and not taking risks. They prefer their secure comfort zones and often become good followers and poor leaders.

A personality makeover can transform them into one of the best leaders. Their sensitivity and patience will make more people want to follow them. Instinctively, they will be kind, but by understanding the benefits of a makeover, they will learn how to be firm. They can become gentle giants.

Some of these personality types will require an "extreme" personality makeover, because they tend to be hesitant. In other words, they will only respond to drastic measures. An "intervention" may be necessary where best friends confront and help this person learn how to control his or her "uniquenesses."

Another extreme measure can be an ongoing mentoring or coaching experience where a friend or counselor monitors the progress and becomes a strong influence. The ultimate goal is to become "all things to all people." Everyone can benefit from the flexibility and adaptation created over time.

With this in mind, someone is bound to ask, "Isn't it wrong to lose our individuality?" Most people think it is not mentally and emotionally healthy to encourage others to lose their identity.

This is NOT about stopping to be who we are!

It is actually becoming what God intended us to be. A makeover is to enhance our personalities and become something we did not realize we could be in order to improve our effectiveness and relationships with others.

As believers in Christ, our identity is in the Lord. We should lose the old self and become new creations in Christ. The old way of thinking, feeling, and acting should be put away. Once we trust Christ as our Savior, He comes into our lives to not only take us to heaven when we die, but to also rearrange the "furniture" of our lives.

He who created the universe wants to recreate a new way of behavior. He desires to redirect the way we reason and analyze things. Christ also yearns to control our feelings and actions. When you exchange faith in yourself with faith in Him for forgiveness and direction in life, you also exchange your personality for His. He wants to control your motivations so they respond *super*naturally, not naturally.

The notion that we must keep our identity and be "ourselves" must go, if we are to have a successful makeover. For some people this is an "extreme" thought, but it is essential to learn. It may not come easy, but it can be accomplished when you understand what Jesus taught: "my work is easy and my burden is light" (Matt. 11:30).

God will never ask you to do anything He won't do for or through you!

When He asks you to have a personality makeover, He will help you. This is not something you have to determine to do. It is not an act of your will in the sense that it is up to you. It is a matter of the will, as you yield to His will in your life. Like someone said, "The heart of the matter is the matter of the heart." God's will is that you allow Him to take control of your personality. He will then make it over into His personality.

Your identity will then be in Him. When people see you, they will notice how your personality reflects Christ in you. Our individuality will be greater and better than ever. We will recognize and see the bigger picture of how God loved us as an individual. He chose to allow us to know Him personally and to control our behavior through our personalities.

*M*ake the decision to have a makeover!

God sees us as unique individuals who trust in Him and obey His Word. Having your own identity will be unnecessary, because your relationship with Christ will overshadow any desire to live without Him. It will no longer be you by yourself having to understand everything. You will no longer be alone to handle all the challenges of life. Once you allow Him to be your Holy Comforter and Counselor — the master of your makeover - you will have His power and personality in you. Your personality will no longer matter. Only His thoughts, feelings, and actions will count.

This is exactly what Jesus did with His humanity when He thought it not "robbery to be equal with God, but emptied Himself, took on the form of a servant and became obedient unto death" (Phil. 2:6-7). He died to His human will and obeyed His Father. He emptied Himself of His natural thoughts, feelings, and actions. It is His human personality yielded to His divine calling that made the difference.

Transformation Is More Important Than Temperament

An extreme personality makeover can do the same for you. Every believer needs to recognize that holding on to our old self and demanding our individuality or identity will rob us of the new and better way. As we yield to God's divine design, our personalities will be made over and transformed into dynamic influences for God's glory. It may also make us into something we are not now, but someone God desires us to be.

The issue of identity and individuality will no longer be important, because we will be clothed in His righteousness and wrapped in His personality. *Who* we are will not be as important as *Whose* we are. It will no longer be about us and our individual motivations. It will be about Him and the personality He wants us to be at any given time or place.

God desires to have us "put on the new man, which is renewed in knowledge after the image that created him" (Col. 3:10). We are to become Christ-like, not like a specific personality type. Once we understand this principle, it will not matter what our personalities are. We will then be free to respond with whatever behavior people need from us according to God's will and way.

This can truly be an "extreme" experience — beyond our furthest dreams.

It can be more than we ever imagined and more than our greatest expectations. Scripture promises, "Eyes have not seen, nor ears heard, neither has it entered into the mind of man, the things God has prepared for those who love Him (1 Cor. 2:9). This can be one of the most exciting experiences of your life!

You should pause and pray that you will let God have His way in your life. Claim His promise to do it through you (Phil. 4:13). Visualize the results of your personality makeover, and expect one of the most exciting learning experiences ever.

Let the makeover begin!

2
*A*ccept The "Way" God Made Your Personality!

Certain people say, "I don't like my personality." Others respond, "I don't like it either." We tend to like or dislike our personalities. This great contrast is because people do not realize that everyone has a good personality because God created it. Most people have concluded there are favorable and unfavorable personality types.

These concepts started when we were very young. Our parents and relatives would comment on how friendly or shy we were. Though this has little to do with forming our personality, it influenced our thinking. It redefined what was already in us and the value of certain types became cloudy. We were conditioned to think outgoing people were better than withdrawn types.

Then in middle and senior high school, we experienced obvious acceptance or rejection based upon our personalities. There were awards for "most friendly," "most popular," and even "best personality." We were scarred for life with this value system that rated personalities from best to worst.

There is even an "oldie-goldie" tune, "*She's got personality*" that vocalized, "She's got walk, talk, and a great big smile." It implies those with effervescent and expressive personalities have it, whatever "it" is.

Then there was the "*Duke of Earl*" song. He seemed to be so powerful and strong that "no one could touch" him. And what about "*Sweet little Susie*" - the opposite of the "Duke?" Everybody loved Susie because she was so sweet. On the other hand, "*Charlie Brown was a clown*." There are so many examples of how songs reflect our feelings about ourselves.

There are other songs that jump out at us, like "you talk too much, you worry me to death" and "grumble, grumble, grumble." Each one seems to express different personality types. Of course as Christians, our favorite songs are now the hymns and choruses that touch our soul and spirit.

As a side note, I reviewed the lyrics of today's (7/5/05) top 10 secular songs and was shocked by the overwhelming sexual references expressed. Perversion has not really changed from my generation to now, but is currently so obviously rotten. Many of the songs I heard as a teen in the early 1960s were also meaningless and tasteless, but it seems today's flavors are much more bitter and poisonous.

The point is that our personalities have affected and influenced our feelings about our personalities. Society obviously has misconceptions that some personalities are better than others.

Personalities by themselves are "amoral!"

In other words, they are without morality, neither good nor bad. Like our hands, they have no sense of right and wrong. It is what we do with our hands that can be judged as moral or not.

To say that someone has a "bad personality" is incorrect. We can say an individual uses his or her personality in bad ways, but the personality itself is not evil. It is how it is used that matters. Our personalities were created as impartial tools to relate and respond to life as we choose.

We can use these tools in right and wrong ways, but to suggest the tool itself is bad is not accurate. The tool can be developed to be used criminally, but that is a totally different subject.

The criminal can choose to use their personality for evil, but to suggest there is a definite criminal personality may be a misconception. The personality itself is not criminal, but evil people use their personalities in terrible ways.

*A*ccept The "Way" God Made Your Personality!

Keep in mind, everyone has a propensity toward evil. You do not have to teach a baby to deceive. Children learn to lie at a very early age. Scripture teaches that we were all conceived with a sin nature (Psa. 51:5). We all, because of our old nature, have the potential to develop a criminal mind or "personality."

This may seem confusing, but think of how most people's minds were born without major presumptions. Apart from our I.Q. (Intelligent Quotient), E.Q. (Emotional Quotient), and / or E.I. (Emotional Intelligence), our minds were born with a blank slate when it comes to knowledge and experiences. (There is evidence that babies in the womb are affected by noises, drugs, and other outside influences, but that is a deeper subject than we need to consider now.)

Our minds were also designed with the ability to absorb knowledge. As we grew, our minds began to develop good and bad habits of thinking and processing the experiences that touched our lives.

Nature vs. Nurture

Some people believe there are certain physical characteristics of criminals' minds that cause them to have a propensity toward very evil acts. This may or may not be true, but our personalities are more like normal minds when we come into the world. Our personality has a certain structure with special ways of thinking, feeling, and acting. Everything we experience from birth to adolescence seems to develop our personalities into the people we become.

In other words, we are conceived with a sin nature, plus a special personality coding and mapping feature. Our early childhood experiences also form us into the people we become. It is a combination of "nature" (divine design) and "nurture" (the growing-up process) that influences who we become.

Do not confuse our sin nature with our personalities. They are two different influences. Our sin nature came from Adam's disobedience and it influences our behavior. Our personalities are neither good nor bad, but are influenced by our natural selves.

The remedy to sin is salvation. The best thing that can happen to our personality is to be controlled by God once we come to know Him. Without a personal relationship with Christ, our sin nature is prone to selfishness and greed. Our personalities, when left alone, are susceptible to sin's power in our lives. We tend toward decay, degeneration and misdirection without God, because of the Law of Entropy and the consequences of sin.

The Lord made our personalities to know and glorify Him. Regeneration by faith in the finished work of Christ creates new life in us and our personalities. We are then free to live beyond ourselves and develop our personalities to their fullest as God originally intended.

God gave us different personalities so we would glorify Him through His controlling power within. If we had all the personality traits evident in our lives, no one would see the differences God can make.

We are living Epistles, known and read of all people (2 Cor. 3:2)!

People are reading our lives everyday. The best way for others to see God's work in our lives is how we control our behavior. We are never more influential then when pressure attacks us and we let crisis draw us closer to where Christ is.

God purposely gave us different personalities so we can allow Him to be the Lord of our behavior, as well as our only way of going to heaven when we die. We are not saved by works, but

*A*ccept The "Way" God Made Your Personality!

we show our faith by our works. People can not literally see our faith, but they can view the evidence of our faith when we act in ways that show God is in control of our lives.

It is a sign of maturity or spiritual depth when inspiring and enthusiastic personality types show genuine humility. Unbelievers can demonstrate humility, but it is often manipulative and manufactured. When outgoing "people-people" who are true believers in Christ show humility, it is probably because God has broken them to let others shine brighter than they. This is not natural, but can be supernatural.

We were created to be complete in Him!

God also made us "lacking" in our specific personalities so other people would be essential in our lives. God purposely did not give us all the traits of all the personality types so we would need each other. Building relationships helps complete us in Christ.

God has a perfect relationship with the Son and the Spirit as One. So he predetermined we would be one as He is One with the Spirit and Son. If we had all the traits of each of us, there would be no necessity to build relationships with others. No man is an island, and God made us to yearn for deep and abiding relationships with others. He literally makes us over spiritually once we trust Him and grow in relationships with others.

The question now is: "What is our personality type?" The discovery of specific personality types goes back to 400 years before Christ when the respected physician, Hypocrates, observed there seemed to be four distinct types of behavior.

He thought it had something to do with the chemical makeup of our blood and body fluids. His ancient titles are now known as: Choleric, Sanguine, Phlegmatic, and Melancholy. Dr. Tim

LaHaye and Florence Littauer have popularized these types in their books.

William Moulton Marston published his book, "The Emotions of Normal People" in 1928 where he changed the Anglicized Greek titles to simple initials: "D," "I," "S," and "C." This is now known as the "DISC" Model of Human Behavior.

Opposition

Some very conservative Christians reject this scientific explanation of human behavior on the grounds that it is unbiblical. The problem is that this model is neither recommended nor condemned in Scripture. Neither are aerodynamics, computer science, or blood types. They are not mentioned or even hinted at in the Bible.

I have never found a critic of the four Temperaments who has even read Marston's book, much less scientifically investigated it. Many condemn it as though they were scientists, but have no evidence or empirical data from cause and effect proof.

Science is that which has been observed, tested, and proven. It is both observable and repeatable. The "DISC" Model of Human Behavior has been scrutinized and investigated for nearly 2,500 years and stood the test of time. The Scientific Method and peer review have validated its existence.

Everything in the Bible is true, but all truth is not in the Bible. Just because the four Temperaments are not explained in Scriptures does not mean they do not exist. There are numerous scientific discoveries not found in the Bible, but which are now validated and recognized in science.

The "DISC" Model is just a tool. It is not a philosophy or "way of life" to be judged by the Scriptures. It simply makes our way of thinking, feeling, and acting more effective, just like

*A*ccept The "Way" God Made Your Personality!

computers make our lives more efficient.

Taking our blood pressure or checking our cholesterol levels are wise measurements. The Bible reveals nothing about these tools and "tests." Theologians need to stick to the Scriptures and allow scientists to continue their research as long as it does not contradict biblical truth. The scientist Galileo, was also condemned by many of the misguided theologians of his day.

Understanding our personality types in light of what the Bible teaches (about how we should behave) can be extremely enlightening. It can also be very practical.

Critics have a choice!

They can continue to waste their time fighting an established scientific discovery or use science to help themselves and others. They should allow God to use this science to reveal and control their weaknesses ("uniqueness"). Some Christians will argue the validity of personality types, while they continue to overlook their overeating, poor habits, and anger-management.

The Bible has a lot to say about improving our bad attitudes and changing our behavior. Nothing will ever take the place of the Bible, but science can come alongside to help reveal the unknown challenges some people have.

Telling people to not be so "shy" and to let the Holy Spirit control their lack of enthusiasm is good. Once people understand that "shyness" is a personality trait which is neither good nor bad, they can then deal with it more effectively.

Much like using computers to improve our researching and organizing tasks, so Human Behavior Science can enhance our effectiveness. We need to simply accept the way God made us. We should learn how to adapt so we can be more like Christ. We need to be "all things to all people." Enough said!

Discovering your personality type is very easy. You can either complete a short paper instrument that will identify your specific type or you may go online at: *www.uniquelyyou.Net*. Answer a few questions to reveal your personality type. You can also discover it on your own by carefully reading the descriptions of each type and seeing which ones are most and least like you.

To make it as simple as possible, let us visualize a pie or circle divided into two halves. The pie represents all the personality types in one circle. The top half represents all those types who are "Active / Outgoing." They tend to be more optimistic and involved.

Active / Outgoing

They are also known as "extroverts," because they tend to be "outside" themselves and outward as they relate to tasks and people in more positive ways. "Extroverts" are not better than "introverts." They just think they are! (Just joking.)

The upper half of the pie can be divided in half again, into two quarters. Both quarters of the pie are extroverted and outgoing.

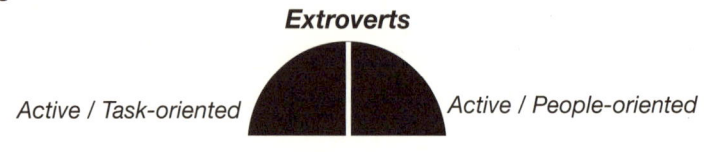

Extroverts

Active / Task-oriented   *Active / People-oriented*

"Extroverts" can be task and people-oriented, or a combination of both. There are those types that are also both "extroverted," as well as "introverted." This is not abnormal. It is just

*A*ccept The "Way" God Made Your Personality!

uncommon.

There is a big difference between "abnormal" and "uncommon." All normal personality types - as opposed to abnormal (neurotic, psychotic, and schizophrenic) types - are typical and ordinary. Some are more familiar than others. In other words, there are some that are more obvious and numerous than other types.

There are more active people-oriented types than there are active task-oriented personalities. That does not make one type better than the other. It is just an observation. One type is more outgoing and involved in getting tasks completed, while the other is more concerned about relationships and influencing people.

The other half of the pie represents the "Passive and Reserved" types.

Passive / Reserved

They are not lesser or lower types. They do not have second class or inferior personalities. This behavior demonstrates a different way of how they view themselves in relationships and tasks. They just show their motivations differently than the "active / outgoing" types.

"Introverts" are "into" themselves. They are more quiet and reserved. They can be people- or task-oriented, or a combination of both. Passive people-oriented types are very loyal and nice. They are not very aggressive or assertive. Pleasing others and creating calm environments motivate them most.

Passive task-oriented individuals are more cautious and calculating, while passive people-oriented types are more sweet and sensitive.

Passive / Task-oriented   *Passive / People-oriented*

Introverts

This is not saying one is better than the other. Every type has its strengths and "uniqueness." All four parts of the pie tend to blend together. Everyone has some or a lot of "D," "I," "S," and "C" behavior. It is all a matter of intensity and how much of each type they have.

We are often affected the most by one or two of the four types. Some people have unique blends of the four, but that only makes them even more unique. No one has a bad blend. The important lesson is identifying our specific type and how it affects our motivations. Now let us look at each one as it stands alone.

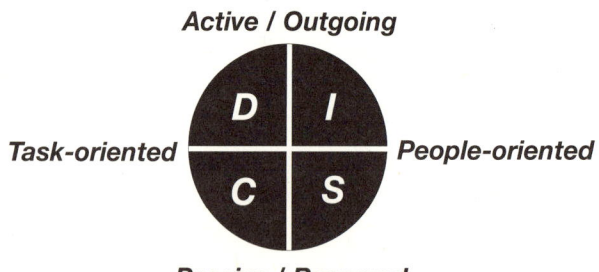

Active / Outgoing

Task-oriented   D | I   **People-oriented**
             C | S

Passive / Reserved

Get this graphic clear in your mind and it will paint a plain picture of the Four Temperament Model of Human Behavior. The Active / Outgoing or "Extroverts" are the "D"s and "I"s, while the Passive / Reserved or "Introverts" are the "S"s and "C"s. They are all equal in value.

We are composites of all four types, but we tend to be more of one or two than the others. It is common to have two stronger traits, while being not as motivated by the others. Each type stands alone with its own recognizable characteristics.

"D" Types

"D" types are more direct, demanding, decisive, and dominant. As active / task-oriented individuals they are determined to get the job done. They are very industrious and forceful. They are strong leaders who like to be bosses.

On the down side, "D"s can be too domineering and demanding. They tend to be impatient and insensitive. They love challenges and strive hard to succeed in accomplishing tasks. "D"s need to guard against the overuse of their strengths.

"I" Types

Influencing and inspiring types are "I"s. They are more exciting and enthusiastic. They love the crowd, the more the merrier. As great communicators, they love to talk. They tend to outshine everyone. Popularity is important to them.

Ego and self-centeredness are their weaknesses. They tend to seek the lime-light. They desire lots of attention and praise. Often upfront and more outgoing than all the other types, they can "steal the show." Humility and quietness are their greatest challenges.

"S" Types

These are the most submissive, sensitive, and soft types. They tend to be more reserved than the others. Their loyal and sweet spirits make them everyone's friends. They often volunteer, not to be seen or recognized, but to simply help others.

People often take advantage of their kindness. They are vulnerable to manipulation and intimidation. Their desire to please makes them seem like weak individuals. They need to speak out and take charge. Ironically, they can be extremely protective when people threaten their loved ones' security.

"C" Type

When you think of the competent, cautious, calculating, careful, and critical thinking types, you are describing "C" types. They have the most conscientious and contemplative personalities. It is not like them to be impulsive or to jump into things. They prefer clear instructions. They are more compliant when it comes to right and wrong. "Going by the book" is one of their strongest motivations.

At the same time, they can be extremely moody and picky. Their concern for correctness often overshadows their care for what people think or feel. They tend to be "loners," disinterested in an exciting social life. Thinking things through often makes them slow decision makers and unbending types.

Each of the "D," I," "S," and "C" types have their strengths and "uniqueness." The following chapters will focus on how each type can have an extreme personality makeover to control their strengths and avoid their weaknesses.

Your goal should be to become more Christ-like and exemplify His work in your life. As you abide in the Vine, His fruit in your life will be the thoughts, feelings, and actions He desires. Your prayer should be like Jesus' plea to the Father, "not my will, but Your will be done" (Luke 22:42)!

3
*K*now your strengths and "uniquenesses."

An extreme personality makeover begins with identifying our specific motivations and predictable patterns of behavior. Once we have a good idea of what makes us tick and what ticks us off, we can then deal with knowing our strengths and "uniquenesses."

Focusing on the "D," "I," "S," and "C" types individually, you can now begin your personality makeover. Keep an open mind and don't let anything discourage you. Some of the comments and insights may seem harsh or strong, but a makeover requires a change of attitude and actions. If you continue through the process, the end results will be worth your effort.

The following are "D" strengths which everyone should exemplify.

"D" Strengths

Asserting	Optimistic	Industrious
Firm	Winner	Hard working
Strong	Competitive	Driving
Bold	Challenging	Determined
Daring	Motivating	Direct
Convinced	Confident	To the point
Decisive	Self-reliant	Devoted
Sure	Persuading	Dedicated
Certain	Convincing	Outspoken
Risk-taking	Serious	Opinionated
Courageous	Unwavering	Zealous
Brave	Powerful	Eager
Adventurous	Unconquerable	Bottom line
Positive		Straight-forward

"D"s are stimulated by the opportunity to accomplish things. They love challenges and choices. They have great confidence and are hard working. They do not like to sit still and do nothing. Depending on their behavioral blend - if they have one - they can be often misunderstood. To improve their effectiveness, they need to guard their strengths and avoid their weaknesses.

"D" Weaknesses ("uniquenesseses")

Identifying someone's weaknesses can be threatening. No one wants to hear about his or her flaws. The key to a successful makeover for "D" types is to recognize the overuse of their good traits can become their weaknesses.

Referring to these traits as "uniquenesses" can be confusing. Actually, what one person calls a weakness is often just a difference in perspective. For example, someone may say a certain "D" type is "too assertive," while another person may say, "I'm so glad they took charge and got the job done. It saved us a lot of time."

A weakness often results from overusing a good thing. Under control, our strengths are considered good traits. "D" types can be "firm" and "strong" with their convictions. To one person it may seem good while to another it may seem bad. People will be impressed and influenced by "D"s' unwavering personalities. Other people will feel safe and secure by "D"s' confidence. The cautious type will even think, "I'm glad someone knows what to do."

Under pressure and stress we lean toward our strengths because that is where we are most confident and comfortable. But the overuse of our strengths become our abuses. We tend to abuse our strengths and overuse the best things about us. The very things people like and fall in love with about us are the

*K*now your strengths and "uniquenesses."

same things they often come to dislike later.

To begin their extreme personality makeover, "D"s should recognize their need to temper their personalities. Interestingly, the word "temper" can be related to "D" types. Just like we "temper" steel to make it stronger, so "D"s must temper their personalities. "D"s want to control everyone, but sometimes can not control themselves. The "bad" side of their personality can be demanding, domineering, cocky, impatient, rude, and forceful.

They tend to be fighters, rather than lovers. Their initial response under pressure is to intimidate and threaten. A personality makeover would be evident when "D"s learn to calmly respond, rather than rudely react. "D"s need to count to 100, rather than 10 before getting mad. It is okay to get mad, but do not do wrong with your anger.

Winners

The word "extreme" is appropriate for "D"s, because they tend to be hot or cold. They despise being on the losing side. They almost never want to be on the losing side of things. They are creatures of extreme. A makeover for them is often major surgery.

Sincere "D"s wanting to be "all things to all people" should first recognize their strengths and weaknesses, then they can deal with their extreme drives to succeed and win in the areas they often fail. Pushing forward comes easy to them, but giving in or letting others be in control comes hard.

Scripture teaches "D"s, "whoever loses their lives will find it" (Mark 8:35). It is a powerful paradox. Think about this: "Keepers weepers. Losers finders." The principle is profound! If you strive to always keep what you have or who you are, you are going to lose in life. If you determine to give yourself away, even if it means losing at times, you will win in life and gain far more than you lose.

To begin your makeover, learn from each of the other personality types. Become more friendly like "I"s. Be kinder and sweeter like "S"s. Make yourself more cautious and careful like "C"s. This may seem unnatural, but it is exactly what you need. Quit making the mistake of thinking "That's not me!" Do you want to be natural or supernatural? You will never be more Christ-like than when you let go and let Him have His way in your life.

Stop thinking that "I"s are "idiots," "S"s are "suckers," and "C"s are "crabby"! "D"s need to become more like "S"s and learn from their strengths. Practice complimenting others and letting them take control of meetings. Submit to your authorities and follow their lead, rather than trying to push your agenda.

Watch how "S"s are more humble and quiet. Be patient and slow down. Do not be the first one to suggest changes or insist to do something. Let others take charge. Be a better follower! Stay calm in difficult situations and control your emotions.

Consequences

Think more about the consequences and consider the options before acting out your passions. Become more like "C"s by researching and evaluating the small details. Do not rely on "gut feelings." Wait, watch, and decide based on the information you gathered before moving forward.

Respect others and do not look down on people. Stop thinking so highly of yourself. Realize that what you are about to do or say affects others. Discipline yourself, rather than telling others what to do. Die to your self will and seek to please Jesus first, Others second, and Yourself last. Then you will have true

K*now your strengths and "uniquenesses."*

JOY.

From a practical perspective, find a friend, mentor, or life-coach to whom you can be accountable. Call them when you struggle with your anger or have anxiety that makes you act poorly at the expense of others. Pay the price for a good counselor or consultant who will keep your feet on the ground. Confess your weakness to God and close friends who can help you. Let them control you. You need someone to hold you accountable to your commitment with your makeover.

You may not like these hard words. If you are not a "D" type it is understandable if you are uncomfortable. You may even take up "D"s' offense and you want to come to their defense. Or you may be glad someone is telling it like it is. You may be thinking: "Give it to 'em. "D"s deserve it!"

But if you are a "D" type, it probably does not bother you. You have heard it before. This extreme makeover may roll right off your back. You may possibly scoff and ridicule the thought that you even need a makeover. That is exactly why you definitely should consider this radical action more than you realize. The question now is: "Do you have the openness to consider a makeover and the will to achieve it?"

To succeed we need to learn from all the different personality types. It will help us adapt in these difficult situations and improve our effectiveness. The following are "I" strengths that should be exemplified in all personalities.

Mels Carbonell, Ph.D

"I" Strengths

Outgoing	Enthusiastic	Sociable
Active	Influencing	Interactive
Playful	Smooth talker	Merry
Fun-loving	Articulate	Cheerful
Delightful	Entertaining	Smiling
Pleasant	Clowning	Happy
Trusting	Admirable	Dynamic
Gullible	Elegant	Impressing
Open	Joyful	Sharp
Friendly	Jovial	Appealing
Cordial	Talkative	Peppy
Popular	Verbal	Playful
Promoting	Animated	Inducing
Encouraging	Expressive	Charming
Hyper	Persuading	Responsive
Energetic	Convincing	Reacting

"I" personalities are perhaps the easiest to convince that makeovers are good, because they are so optimistic. They are also agreeable and encouraging. You will not find many others who are more inspiring and influencing than "I" types.

The "I"s' greatest challenge is controlling their emotions. They tend to be very expressive and feeling-oriented. There is never a dull moment around them. They can be higher than a kite or lower than a skunk, although they tend to be more up than down. You seldom have to wonder what they are thinking or feeling.

They are articulate and have the best communication skills. They seldom think before they speak. "I"s are very good at convincing and influencing others. They tend to be conscious of

*K*now your strengths and "uniquenesses."

their images and usually want to look their best. Sometimes they can be sloppy, because they think their personalities and people-skills will overcome whatever weaknesses they have. They often run late and hurry through their daily schedule. They can throw things together at the last moment and usually get away with it, except with "C" types.

"I" Weaknesses ("uniquenesseses")

Overusing their strengths, "I"s tend to be too self-centered. They often steal the limelight and seek too much attention. When it comes to showing off and making a splash, you can not beat "I" types.

They tend to win awards more than others, because they seek approval and praise. This often causes them to be boastful and proud. Humility is seldom one of their virtues. Noticing the weaknesses or "uniquenesseses" of "I" types is often obvious. They tend to stand out in a crowd.

They often struggle with quietness and stillness. Growing up they can be labeled as hyperactive children. "I"s are also often diagnosed with ADD (Attention Deficit Disorder). Many people with ADD are not "I" types, but most are. Their short attention spans are often misread as problems, rather than positive traits.

"I"s prefer to have fun. They do not like boring or mundane activities. For this reason they are often labeled with having a disorder or weakness. Their strengths are often over-shadowed by their interest in having good times. "I" personalities need to especially guard how they respond to people and tasks.

Their strengths are seen when working with people, while their weaknesses tend to be accomplishing tasks. They would rather "talk" about doing things, rather than actually doing them. They make good impressions and inspire people to work together, but lack determination when it comes to working by themselves and staying at a task until it is done well. They tend to draw back and look for someone to talk to.

"I"s often resist conflict. They would rather take someone out to lunch and "talk it out," rather than go "face to face" with someone who is upset with them. They tend to be negotiators and counselors, rather than confronters.

To be more effective, "I"s should count the cost of looking the other way when they see wrongdoing. They must avoid their weakness of wanting to be everyone's friend. A true friend cares enough to confront.

"I"s also must learn to listen more. They tend to interrupt and want to share their thoughts or feelings. Not listening well is an obvious weakness. They should discipline and control their natural desires to contribute their comments.

A good way to guard against talking too much or constantly interrupting others is to pretend someone is watching or video taping their ability to pay attention. "I"s should imagine a documentary or training film is being produced with them as stars. They should see themselves showing the world, through this film, how to demonstrate interest in others and not themselves.

People Notice

Ironically, people notice how "I"s talk too much and how everything seems to center around them. It is also obvious when "I" types show genuine interest in others. People are more impressed and influenced when "I"s are actually the opposite of what they tend to naturally be.

Desiring praise and glory, "I"s need to constantly remember the principle of "passing on the praise." When complimented, "I"s should pass the glory on to those who allowed them to do

*K*now your strengths and "uniquenesses."

what they do. They should especially pass the praise on to God.

"I" types tend to seek approval and "stroking." They love to shine. They are like mirrors that reflect and radiate light. Mirrors are just reflectors that show the image of something or someone else. Mirrors simply bounce the light off themselves. "I"s must also be reflectors of the glory they receive. They literally outshine others, but often keep the praise they receive and do not pass it on.

God never intended for "I"s to get all the glory!

God resists the proud and gives grace to the humble (Jas. 4:6). He will give His glory to no one (Is. 42:8). "I"s must guard against absorbing and keeping all the praise for themselves. God will tarnish the image of "I" types who hoard the compliments for themselves.

At times, there are many "I" personalities who deserve more praise than they are receiving. But because they are violating the principle of "passing on the praise," God withholds the praise "I"s deserve until they learn to let another man's lips praise them (Prov. 27:2). An extreme personality makeover requires "I"s to focus on the glory of God and lifting others above themselves.

Unfortunately, this can also become a way for "I"s to manipulate their actions and fake their humility. Their interest in others can become another show they put on. God knows their hearts and will ultimately bless or break every "I" who seeks vain glory, rather than build value in others.

"I"s' character, their values within, is more important to them than their reputation. What they do in the darkness will show their character, while what they do in the light in front of others will show their reputation. Character is far more important.

"I"s often get the reputation of being silly and shallow. It has nothing to do with their "I.Q."s, because personality types and intelligence are not related. You can be a typical, flighty "dumb blond" and yet be more intelligent than others. The problem is people associate intelligent people with quiet thinker types.

Impulsive and excitable types are often not considered smart. Right or wrong, "I"s need to guard against giving the impression they are not mentally swift. Learning when to speak and what to say are very important. Cautious and calculated types will often judge the value of what "I"s say by how they say what they say.

> *We've all heard, "it's not what you say, but how you say it that really counts!"*

Learning when and how to say what is important to "I"s is imperative. Guarding their drive to look good and be accepted by everyone are some of the wisest things they can do.

Researching the facts and analyzing the situations will bring more respect to "I"s. Staying calm and sharing their convictions about correctness will really impress others. If "I"s really want to look good and make good impressions, they should think about their actions and reactions. Think before speaking. Analyze before answering. Rehearse before reacting. Prepare before pressing on.

Since "I"s seem to enjoy the spotlight, they should constantly remember people are watching them and evaluating their behavior. Is what others see "all about the "I"s" or do people see Christ in them? The main question in their lives should be: "Who's getting all the glory?"

Seeing how other types deal with these challenges can be very practical. The following are "S" strengths that should be exemplified in all personalities.

*K*now your strengths and "uniquenesses."

"S" Strengths

Kind	Loving	Compassionate
Nice	Sincere	Generous
Caring	Honest	Giving
Gentle	Shy	Timid
Soft	Mild	Soft-spoken
Humble	Diplomatic	Tolerant
Loyal	Peacemaking	Patient
True Blue	Flexible	Serving
Peaceful	Adaptable	Sacrificing
Calm	Agreeable	Courteous
Obedient	Steady	Polite
Submissive	Dependable	Hospitable
Pleasing	Stable	Enjoys company
Good-natured	Balanced	Quiet
Considerate	Merciful	Reserved
Thoughtful	Sensitive	Helpful
Contented	Sweet	Assisting
Satisfied	Tender	

"S"s tend to be the kindest, most gentle people in the world. Their desire to please and serve others makes them so likeable. They do not like to stand out in a crowd, but make great "people-people." They are highly relational in small groups. Loyalty and faithfulness are their hallmarks.

Some people think "S"s are anti-social, because they tend to be quieter than others. "S"s are more shy, but are also sociable among close friends. Their greatest strengths are their patient and sensitive spirits.

They can be gentle giants as leaders. As diplomatic and compassionate types, they are more tolerant and flexible. They do not like to be forceful or demanding.

People enjoy "S"s because they are so considerate and humble. They do not tend to compete for attention, but would rather let others get the praise they may deserve. They are thoughtful and faithful friends to the end.

"S" Weaknesses ("uniquenesses")

Others often take advantage of "S"s merciful demeanor. "S"s are prey for people looking for someone who is easy to manipulate. They need to be more resistant of those who try to use them. "S" types can also become "codependent."

In other words, they can become too dependent on others. This dependency can cripple them. They do not want to make any major decisions. "S"s need to be more assertive and learn to say "no" when others try to intimidate them.

To have a successful makeover, "S"s must learn to be more outgoing. This will seem very unnatural for them, but it is so imperative. Being outgoing does not mean being friendlier. They are already friendly, almost to a fault. They need to be more outgoing to the crowd, as well as to the individual.

In other words, "S"s should jump into conversations and share what they think or feel about the subject being discussed. "S" types tend to quietly listen while others dominate the conversations. Their attentive responses encourage others to keep talking. "S"s should interrupt and add their thoughts. They need to control their desire to please and be more aggressive.

Dominant types single out "S"s as their "slaves." Once a pattern is established, it is hard for "S"s to stand up to arrogant strong types. Notice we are not referring to "stronger" types. Everyone is strong in their own way. Some people are strong when it comes to completing tasks, while others are strong when

*K*now your strengths and "uniquenesses."

it comes to relating to others.

Driven and determined personalities consider themselves stronger than "S"s, but actually the "D"s' strengths become their weaknesses when it comes to building relationships. "S"s are much stronger in the caring and sharing needs. This also makes them vulnerable to those who prey on their nurturing interests.

Their good will is often abused. "S"s must learn to be stronger in potential conflicts. They need to stand up for themselves and not let people push them around. Ironically "S"s can act just like "D"s when someone threatens their families. Like protective mother hens, "S"s can explode and act like a madperson if you try to hurt their kids or disrupt their comfort zones.

Everyone has a bell or button that once pushed or ringed, makes them come out fighting. They can be like bulls in china closets or bulldozers. Surprisingly, they can act just like "D"s out of control. Their personality makeover involves their conscientious efforts to control their potential out-of-control behavior when threatened.

On one hand, "S"s should be more aggressive, but under extreme pressure they need to guard their passions to protect. Their need for stability and security often makes them very careful and resistant to changes. They do not like change for change's sake. They prefer stable and steady environments.

Thinking Things Through

Another important behavior "S"s should consider improving is their thinking things through. They are not contemplative or thorough investigators about the facts and figures. Researching and in-depth analysis are recommended in their makeover. If you are an "S" type, pause and ask, "Should I do this because it makes sense or am I doing this just to please someone?"

Evaluating motives will be powerful and practical. "S"s are not usually aggressive and seldom initiate tasks. It is not because they are thinking the process through, but rather they may be hesitant to try new and daring things.

"S"s should try to be more entrepreneurial and take added risks. They should first count the costs, then try new things. They should also learn to be more persuasive and promoting. When "S"s get excited about something other than their grandchildren or winning something big, people take notice. It is not characteristic for "S"s to be really enthusiastic or vibrant. They actually have better results than other types, because people do not expect them to be so excited.

Once "S"s have completed their makeover, they will make great impressions on everyone. They will be more effective and accomplish much more for God's glory.

Everyone should seriously review why and what they do to improve their relationships and results. The following are "C" strengths that should be exemplified in all personalities.

Know your strengths and "uniquenesses."

"C" Strengths

Proper	Correct	Researching
Formal	Competent	Systematic
Law-abiding	Does right	Follows plan
Conscientious	Contemplative	Inquisitive
Calculating	Thinker	Questioning
Analytical	Deep	Original
Conservative	Intense	Creative
Inflexible	Perceptive	Strict
Careful	Sees clearly	Unbending
Cautious	Pondering	Inventive
Straight	Wondering	Imaginative
Conforming	Guarded	Organized
Compliant	Masked	Orderly
Goes by book	Protective	Faithful
Right	Preparing	Consistent

"C" type personalities are the most cautious and calculating types. If you want something done correctly, give it to "C" types. The challenge will arise when they complain that they do not have enough time or resources. They always want to accomplish the task the way *they* think it should be completed.

"C"s are often respected for their reasoning skills. They tend to ask the important and difficult questions other people overlook. They need lots of information to formulate their opinions. As slow decision-makers, they can be either irritating or comforting to others.

They are valuable to groups, but often prefer to work alone. Their inquisitiveness and "pickiness" are so necessary when it comes to research and development. "C"s tend to be more task-than people-oriented. They prefer quiet and stress-free environments. People often refer to them as "loners" and accuse them of not having a personality. Of the four personality types, "C"s will probably benefit the most from having a personality makeover.

"C" Weaknesses ("uniquenesses")

Their desire for perfection often makes them difficult people to relate to. They tend to care more about propriety than people. Being correct is often more important than being close. Their attitudes can come across as being superior to others.

People are often threatened by "C"s because they seem to be arrogant and quick to judge. They tend to be more right than wrong, but they need to be more forgiving and understanding. One of their greatest frustrations is dealing with people who are sloppy or disorganized. "C"s can be too hard and unkind.

They especially need to learn how to be more sensitive to other people's feelings. Instead of focusing on the facts or details, they should consider how people are going to respond to their judgments. "C" types would be more effective if they would judge themselves more than judging others.

They tend to be cold and unapproachable. Being warm and friendly does not come naturally to them. They should learn to be more positive and excited about other people's ideas. "C"s come across as boring and dull types, except to other "C"s.

They may have tremendous feelings for others, but do not show them easily. They can be very faithful, but it usually revolves around a task or responsibility. They tend to be very conscientious. They like to do one thing at a time, but can become impatient with those who seem incompetent.

"C"s strive to go "by-the-book." In other words, they demand that everyone abide by the rules. The policies and proce-

Know your strengths and "uniquenesses."

dures stated or written must be obeyed. They do not like to cut corners or do the minimum required. They conclude that it is a matter of doing things right or not doing them at all. As "picky-perfectionists," they can be too hard on themselves and others.

They need to loosen up and be more upbeat. Looking for the good and not the bad in things is recommended for most "C"s. Caring more about people's feelings than their accuracy will make super impressions on others. Their makeover must include improving their people skills.

Communication

Speaking out with enthusiasm and positive attitudes will greatly enhance their effectiveness. Learning how to communicate with "gusto" and high energy is often more important than what they say. People will be convinced sometimes more by the "style" than the "substance" of what "C"s say.

They need to add more "sugar" to their presentations and conversations. Letting their hair down will shout volumes more than the information they feel compelled to share. People will actually learn more through "C"s' enthusiasm and excitement, rather than their deep and boring lessons.

Adding direct and decisive conclusions to their sharing and teaching will create more attention and interest. Being obviously impressive and aggressive as confident leaders will pay off in the long run.

As competent critics, "C" types are often harder on themselves than others. They tend to become depressed and pessimistic. They call it being "concerned," not "worried." They should "count their blessings" and look at the positive side of problems.

They can also be too hard on those they are closest to. Familiarity often breeds contempt and the closer they are to people, the harder they can be on them. They often struggle with intimate relationships.

At work, they tend to move away from people into their own "task" worlds. As leaders, they can be impossible to please. Their demand for excellence is often impossible. "C"s make the best teachers when they are patient and enthusiastic.

Perfection

They must guard their constant pushing for perfection. Most people do not like working under "C"s because of their apparent lack of feelings. Ironically, they can be very caring, but do not show it well. Their personality makeover will definitely include improving their people-skills.

The best thing "C"s could do to enhance their relationships and effectiveness is to show genuine concern for others. Instead of always focusing on what needs to be done or how to correct something, they should stop for a moment and ask others how they (others) are feeling. They should demonstrate more care for the person than the project.

"C"s will draw more out of people, once they show obvious concern for others' needs, rather than sharing their passion for the pressing task. "C" personalities' most obvious challenges will be in the work verses worker decisions. Sometimes tasks are more important, but most of the time building relationships should be their priority.

Once you have identified your specific personality with its strengths and weaknesses ("uniquenesses"), you can become more sensitive to your predictable patterns of behavior. Keep in mind, most people are blends of "D," "I," "S," and "C" types. For example, they can be "D/C"s, "I/S"s, or "S/C"s etc. It does not matter what your type is. What really counts is the personali-

Know your strengths and "uniquenesses."

ties of others and how you adapt to their needs. Learn to respond to people according to how they think, feel, and act to improve your effectiveness.

Practical Application

Everyone has their challenges. What comes easy for one type can be very difficult for another. We need to guard against thinking too highly of our personalities and feeling bad about our shortcomings. You are a valuable person in God's plan for others. You can be an example to follow and you can learn from others what to do or avoid.

The key to applying what you are learning is being aware of what is happening as you relate to people. Then adapt and improve your drives so you can what they person and what you need to be.

Humorously, I just heard from a good friend who has a lot of "S" qualities in his personality. He was listening to his super-high "I" sister for over an hour just talking endlessly about anything that came to her mind. After so long of listening, he decided to share his thoughts.

He proceeded to talk and after a couple of minutes he looked at his sister and she was fast asleep. He smiled and thought to himself that she needed the rest after talking so long. So much for two-sided conversations.

His sister is one of the most enthusiastic and encouraging ladies in the world, but boy can she talk. My friend is so patient and kind that he allows her to exercise her personality's strengths. He is also mature enough to know when he should speak and decided to share (to no avail), but at least he tried.

If you are an "I" type watch yourself talking. Ask questions to draw people into the conversation. If you are a "S" type, interrupt and force yourself into conversations. If you are a "D" type guard your forcefulness and be kinder and more gentle under pressure. If you are a "C" type, relax and have more fun by laughing and smiling more. We all have our "uniqueness" and should trust the Lord to turn our weaknesses into strengths.

4

*E*mulate the good traits of all the personality types.

An Extreme Personality Makeover must include accepting the way God made you and knowing your strengths and uniquenesses. Once you grasp those two important handles, you should then learn how to emulate the good traits of all the personality types. Your makeover will succeed or fail based on how you lift yourself out of your "routine" behavior.

Everyone has a predictable pattern of behavior that reveals their specific personality type. We often respond to life's challenges in ways that are easiest for us. The opposite responses are harder because they do not seem natural. We often feel uncomfortable acting, thinking, or feeling differently than how we are wired.

The key to becoming "all things to all people" and improving our effectiveness, is not caving into our cravings or tendencies, but instead controlling our natural desires. This may sound strange, but it is how God works in our lives. The Laws of Physics teaches that for every action, there is an equal and opposite reaction.

When we "go with the flow" and let our "feelings be our guide," it is easier, but we often get into trouble. When we "think past the present" and do what is wise, we often avoid serious consequences. When we do what is supernatural, that which is often opposite of what is natural, we counter our natural reactions with wise decisions.

Therefore, we must master the good traits of the other personality types. Success often flows from the fountain of imitation, rather than replication. We often do not learn from our mistakes. The one thing we definitely learn from history, is we do not learn from history!

History

History is actually "His Story!" All of history revolves around Christ's story. From B.C. to A.D., His story is the central theme of time. Christ is the focal point of life. Our history should be "His Story" in all we say and do. His saving life and controlling power should be our story to a lost and dying world. "By Him, we live, move, and have our being," (Acts 17:28).

Nothing will shout this truth louder than when we believe Jesus not only paid for our sins, but He also can improve our behavior. Some Christians get trapped by thinking that grace is a license to sin, when in reality it is a liberty and open door to live the Christ-like life.

We have been saved from the penalty of sin. We are also being saved from the power of sin in our lives and someday we will eventually be saved from the very presence of sin when we go to heaven.

The problem is, we have to live in a world that is a friend of our flesh and selfishness. We want to run our own lives. We want to be the captain of our ships and masters of our fates. The desire to decide for ourselves how to think, feel, and act is self-destructive. It tells a story of spiritual tragedy.

The life that condones selfishness and the right to act naturally, rather than spiritually, leads to decay and disaster. We must learn to emulate the good traits of others to counterbalance our natural traits.

This is not to imply our normal way of thinking, feeling, and acting is bad or always wrong. There are many good qualities we possess. But when left alone and not guarded, our good traits often turn into overuses. We tend to go too far with our natural

*E*mulate the good traits of all the personality types!

feelings and thoughts, turning our actions into abuses. Our good traits turn into bad behavior when not controlled.

"I" Behavior "D"s Need To Learn

The following are examples of "I" personality traits that may not come naturally to "D"s. We need to emulate these behaviors. For example, "D" types should develop more "I" behavior. If you are a "D" type, think about how each of these behaviors are - or are not - part of your life:

Playful	Merry	Smooth talker
Fun-loving	Cheerful	Articulate
Delightful	Smiling	Entertaining
Pleasant	Happy	Clowning
Trusting	Dynamic	Admirable
Gullible	Impressing	Elegant
Open	Sharp	Joyful
Friendly	Appealing	Jovial
Cordial	Peppy	Talkative
Popular	Playful	Verbal
Encouraging	Inducing	Animated
Hyper	Charming	Expressive
Energetic	Responsive	Persuading
Sociable	Enthusiastic	Convincing
Interactive	Influencing	

Honestly ask yourself if you demonstrate these types of behaviors when you are stressed and forced into a corner. What comes out of you when people poke you like the happy television character, "Pillsbury Doughboy?" Or are you like the "Incredible Hulk" turning into a monster when things do not go your way? Do you explode and stretch the limits of people's emotions?

As a "D" type, seriously look at each of the previous adjectives and determine to learn how to be like them. In other words, be more playful and fun loving instead of being so serious. When things are disorganized and everyone seems to be aimlessly lost in having a good time, join in. Do not start barking orders and try to drive the group toward more results-oriented tasks.

Let your hair down and have some fun. Life is too short. You will probably make a big impression on the crowd and the next time you have the opportunity to lead they will be more responsive to you. Guard yourself before you explode or say something offensive. Control your feelings and do not intimidate the group into moving toward what you think is more constructive activity.

Take each of the "I"s' traits and think through how you can learn from them. Sit back some day and observe "I"s in action. Instead of thinking poorly of them, admire their abilities to influence and impress others through their excitement and enthusiasm.

Also consider learning from "S"s. This will probably be your hardest behavior to emulate. "D"s often view "S"s as weak types. Driving and determined types often think sweet and sensitive types are too meek and soft.

*E*mulate the good traits of all the personality types!

"S" Behavior "D"s Need To Learn

Look at the following "S" behaviors and think of how "D"s can improve through each of them.

Kind	Loving	Compassionate
Nice	Sincere	Generous
Caring	Honest	Giving
Gentle	Shy	Timid
Soft	Mild	Soft-spoken
Humble	Diplomatic	Tolerant
Loyal	Peacemaking	Patient
True Blue	Flexible	Serving
Peaceful	Adaptable	Sacrificing
Calm	Agreeable	Courteous
Obedient	Steady	Polite
Submissive	Dependable	Hospitable
Pleasing	Stable	Enjoys company
Good-natured	Balanced	Quiet
Considerate	Merciful	Reserved
Thoughtful	Sensitive	Helpful
Contented	Sweet	Assisting
Satisfied	Tender	

For example, how kind are you as a "D" type? Do you let other people cut in line without you getting mad or saying anything? Can you be nice to someone who is being mean to you or do you feel compelled to fight back? Try exchanging good for evil, showing interest in those who do not care, and being gentle when you think you should be hard or forceful.

"C" behavior is also extremely important to learn. It is task-oriented, but in a passive way. As an active task focused person "D"s should look beyond what is expedient to that which is excellent. The following are important traits "D"s should learn to emulate from "C" types.

"C" Behavior "D"s Need To Learn

Proper	Correct	Researching
Formal	Competent	Systematic
Law-abiding	Does Right	Follows plan
Conscientious	Contemplative	Inquisitive
Calculating	Thinker	Questioning
Analytical	Deep	Original
Conservative	Intense	Creative
Inflexible	Perceptive	Strict
Careful	Sees clearly	Unbending
Cautious	Pondering	Inventive
Straight	Wondering	Imaginative
Conforming	Guarded	Organized
Compliant	Masked	Orderly
Goes by book	Protective	Faithful
Right	Preparing	Consistent

For example, "D"s should always stop and think about the consequences of their quick responses. They should slow down and determine to not make a rash or improper decision. Instead of pulling the trigger on a task and finishing it faster than anyone else, "D"s should be more cautious and calculating. Analysis from a long-term perspective will protect "D"s from foolish and unwise actions.

*E*mulate the good traits of all the personality types!

"D" Behavior "I"s Need To Learn

"I" personalities should also emulate "D" types. This may be difficult to imagine, because "I"s often have the attitude they have the best personalities and do not need to learn from anyone. That is one of their biggest mistakes. If you are an "I" type, review the following traits and see how you can improve your so-called "perfect" personality.

Asserting	Optimistic	Hard working
Firm	Winner	Driving
Strong	Competitive	Determined
Bold	Challenging	Direct
Daring	Motivating	To the point
Convinced	Confident	Devoted
Decisive	Self-reliant	Dedicated
Sure	Persuading	Outspoken
Certain	Convincing	Opinionated
Risk-taking	Serious	Zealous
Courageous	Unwavering	Eager
Brave	Powerful	Bottom line
Adventurous	Unconquerable	Straight-forward
Positive	Industrious	

For example, "I" types can be great at negotiating and communicating, but should improve their assertiveness. They often back off in tough situations. This can be good and bad depending on the seriousness of the outcome. "I"s often care more about having lots of friends than doing the right thing or winning the battle.

They need to learn from "D" types how to be bold and brave, regardless what the crowd thinks. This can be very dangerous. "I"s need to be sure that standing firm and being strong against opposition is the right thing to do. The consequences can be serious. The cost can be expensive. Having friends and being popular is not always best.

At the same time, "I"s are very good at reading people. Their greatest challenges will be standing up to "D" and "C" types who will not buy "I"s' enthusiasm and excitement.

"S" Behavior "I"s Need To Learn

The following are "S" traits that "I" types should emulate.

Kind	Loving	Compassionate
Nice	Sincere	Generous
Caring	Honest	Giving
Gentle	Shy	Timid
Soft	Mild	Soft-spoken
Humble	Diplomatic	Tolerant
Loyal	Peacemaking	Patient
True Blue	Flexible	Serving
Peaceful	Adaptable	Sacrificing
Calm	Agreeable	Courteous
Obedient	Steady	Polite
Submissive	Dependable	Hospitable
Pleasing	Stable	Enjoys company
Good-natured	Balanced	Quiet
Considerate	Merciful	Reserved
Thoughtful	Sensitive	Helpful
Contented	Sweet	Assisting
Satisfied	Tender	

Just like "D"s needing to be more like "S"s, "I" types should pursue the same goals to practice "S" behavior. "I"s tend to be manipulators. They can act like "S"s to get what they want. Life

*E*mulate the good traits of all the personality types!

has a way of evening the score, and "I"s reap what they sow when they are crafty and complimentary for self gain.

"I"s are the best actors and sometimes put on a good show of caring for others. Acting like "S"s comes easy, because "I"s are also people-oriented. Their greatest challenge will be sincerity. Learning to care with no expectation or reward will be difficult for "I"s. Emulating "S"s sweet and unselfish behavior will be "I"s most applauding achievements.

"C" Behavior "I"s Need To Learn

The following "C" traits can be the most difficult for "I" types.

Proper	Correct	Researching
Formal	Competent	Systematic
Law-abiding	Does Right	Follows plan
Conscientious	Contemplative	Inquisitive
Calculating	Thinker	Questioning
Analytical	Deep	Original
Conservative	Intense	Creative
Inflexible	Perceptive	Strict
Careful	Sees clearly	Unbending
Cautious	Pondering	Inventive
Straight	Wondering	Imaginative
Conforming	Guarded	Organized
Compliant	Masked	Orderly
Goes by book	Protective	Faithful
Right	Preparing	Consistent

Since "I" types tend to be more "feelers" than "thinkers," having to calculate and contemplate can stretch their limits. Often giddy and humorous, "I"s give the impression of being shallow. To improve their effectiveness, they should pause and ponder their actions and possible consequences.

Their temptation will be to put on a show for others. They are master manipulators and will eventually be trapped by their own deceit, if they do not learn to seriously consider the facts and plan their work.

"D" Behavior "S"s Need To Learn

The following "D" traits often seem impossible for "S"s.

Asserting	Optimistic	Hard working
Firm	Winner	Driving
Strong	Competitive	Determined
Bold	Challenging	Direct
Daring	Motivating	To the point
Convinced	Confident	Devoted
Decisive	Self-reliant	Dedicated
Sure	Persuading	Outspoken
Certain	Convincing	Opinionated
Risk-taking	Serious	Zealous
Courageous	Unwavering	Eager
Brave	Powerful	Bottom line
Adventurous	Unconquerable	Straight-forward
Positive	Industrious	

It will be very difficult for sweet, soft, and sensitive types to act like demanding, driving, and decisive types. It is just not their style, but that does not mean "S"s cannot learn how to "swim with the sharks," as one author put it. It can be survival of the fittest, "do it or die" when it comes to handling those who constantly intimidate you.

"S"s have the sweetest personalities, but often become prey

*E*mulate the good traits of all the personality types!

for those who look for someone to control. "S"s can stand firm when pushed too far, but need to not wait till that time comes. They should initiate, then close the deal. "S"s should take charge and tell people what to do without being rude or controlling.

Their sweet demeanor combined with assertive behavior will surprise people, but it will also results in highly effective action.

"I" Behavior "S"s Need To Learn

"S"s should also learn from the "I" types. Consider these traits as you complete your extreme personality makeover.

Playful	Merry	Smooth talker
Fun-loving	Cheerful	Articulate
Delightful	Smiling	Entertaining
Pleasant	Happy	Clowning
Trusting	Dynamic	Admirable
Gullible	Impressing	Elegant
Open	Sharp	Joyful
Friendly	Appealing	Jovial
Cordial	Peppy	Talkative
Popular	Playful	Verbal
Encouraging	Inducing	Animated
Hyper	Charming	Expressive
Energetic	Responsive	Persuading
Sociable	Enthusiastic	Convincing
Interactive	Influencing	

Acting out of character is wrong, but responding with flexibility is powerful. We do not have to deny who we are when we choose to be wise and change our natural course of action. "S"s really struggle with trying to be something they are not, but they should remember how they can act when really pressured.

"S"s can make great actors and dynamic communicators when they understand their resistance within. Overcoming shyness and becoming the personality they need to be will cause them to be more influential and impressive.

"C" Behavior "S"s Need To Learn

"S"s should also take on "C" traits when necessary. The following are suggestions for "S"s to learn.

Proper	Correct	Researching
Formal	Competent	Systematic
Law-abiding	Does Right	Follows plan
Conscientious	Contemplative	Inquisitive
Calculating	Thinker	Questioning
Analytical	Deep	Original
Conservative	Intense	Creative
Inflexible	Perceptive	Strict
Careful	Sees clearly	Unbending
Cautious	Pondering	Inventive
Straight	Wondering	Imaginative
Conforming	Guarded	Organized
Compliant	Masked	Orderly
Goes by book	Protective	Faithful
Right	Preparing	Consistent

"S"s are much like "C" types, because they are both passive. "S" personalities are more people-oriented, than "C"s; therefore, they seek to please in their serving, rather than getting the task done right, regardless of what others think. "S"s are the most faithful and consistent when it comes to work, but are not as driven toward perfection as "C"s are.

*E*mulate the good traits of all the personality types!

If "S" types focused more on correction and quality, they would make great leaders. Their commitment to people needs to be balanced with their concern for organization and preparing without being told to do so.

"D" Behavior "C"s Need To Learn

"C" personalities would benefit from "D"s by learning the following traits.

Asserting	Optimistic	Hard working
Firm	Winner	Driving
Strong	Competitive	Determined
Bold	Challenging	Direct
Daring	Motivating	To the point
Convinced	Confident	Devoted
Decisive	Self-reliant	Dedicated
Sure	Persuading	Outspoken
Certain	Convincing	Opinionated
Risk-taking	Serious	Zealous
Courageous	Unwavering	Eager
Brave	Powerful	Bottom line
Adventurous	Unconquerable	Straight-forward
Positive	Industrious	

It is perhaps hardest for "C"s to have a personality makeover, because they tend to be strict and systematic. Ironically, they can also be very imaginative and creative. They make great character actors, because they can immerse themselves into another person's life.

Their ability to mask (in a good way) their true feelings and thoughts can come across with convincing and confident behavior. "C"s should think through this makeover idea and learn to adapt to each of the personality types to improve their effectiveness.

They do not need to be trapped in the stereotype of being seen as "moody melancholies" or "nerds." They can become strong, positive, and to the point leaders. They do not have to be as thorough or prepared as they think. Learn to be spontaneous and "wing it" with confidence when you have to.

"I" Behavior "C"s Need To Learn

"C"s should also learn from the "I" types. The following are "I" traits to adapt.

Playful	Merry	Smooth talker
Fun-loving	Cheerful	Articulate
Delightful	Smiling	Entertaining
Pleasant	Happy	Clowning
Trusting	Dynamic	Admirable
Gullible	Impressing	Elegant
Open	Sharp	Joyful
Friendly	Appealing	Jovial
Cordial	Peppy	Talkative
Popular	Playful	Verbal
Encouraging	Inducing	Animated
Hyper	Charming	Expressive
Energetic	Responsive	Persuading
Sociable	Enthusiastic	Convincing
Interactive	Influencing	

As thinkers first and foremost, "C"s should recognize how "one type fits all" does not work when it comes to effectiveness. Adapting to the needs of each individual fits best for all. Instead of being typically serious and cold, "C"s should interact and

*E*mulate the good traits of all the personality types!

articulate their enthusiasm.

Become contagious and charming like "I" types. Be pleasant and cheerful when things don't go as planned. Bend and encourage more. Learn from the "I"s how to be happy and don't worry about the small and "big" stuff.

"S" Behavior "C"s Need To Learn

"C"s should also learn from "S"s. The following are "S" traits to emulate.

Kind	Loving	Compassionate
Nice	Sincere	Generous
Caring	Honest	Giving
Gentle	Shy	Timid
Soft	Mild	Soft-spoken
Humble	Diplomatic	Tolerant
Loyal	Peacemaking	Patient
True Blue	Flexible	Serving
Peaceful	Adaptable	Sacrificing
Calm	Agreeable	Courteous
Obedient	Steady	Polite
Submissive	Dependable	Hospitable
Pleasing	Stable	Enjoys company
Good-natured	Balanced	Quiet
Considerate	Merciful	Reserved
Thoughtful	Sensitive	Helpful
Contented	Sweet	Assisting
Satisfied	Tender	

"C"s tend to be the most thought provoking and analytical types. Becoming like "S"s can be easy from a passive perspective, but it will be difficult from a task perspective. Learning to adjust their thinking to "S" types will make "C"s more effective.

Instead of focusing on getting a task done correctly, "C"s should think more about the people they are working with and how to build closer relationships. "C"s need to relax and be satisfied with the pace, to be more forgiving and tolerant of other peoples' feelings and thinking.

If you noticed each of the traits for every type was similar, it is because there are typical traits every personality type should learn. These are not the only traits. There are many more you may want to add to each list. Take a moment to think through the traits you lack. Then add them to your list.

Keep in mind most people are blends.

We have focused on each type individually. When you add a blend or two to the mix this creates a whole new set of requirements for a personality makeover. Consider your blend and how whatever you are lacking can be adapted to your life style.

Become so efficient at reading people and recognizing how to be flexible so people will not be able to tell what personality you have. *This is revolutionary thinking.* It struggles against the idea of wanting to be "ourselves," but is biblical and wise thinking.

Stop demanding to be what you are and allow God to make you what He wants you to be — "all things to all people!" When you allow Him to do it through you, it will be a healthy and happy experience.

Start slow with little changes here and there. Then work up to the extreme differences that may really challenge your ability to adapt. This makeover can work, if you work at it. Be conscious of your initial responses and guard yourself from overusing your strengths.

*E*mulate the good traits of all the personality types!

Pay more attention to your weaknesses. Let God "finish" His work in you (Phil. 1:6) by turning your weaknesses into strengths. Just like expensive "Finishing Schools" teach children to be proper, learn to emulate all the good personality traits.

Also imagine yourself as a newly discovered beautiful diamond. The Master Craftsman, God, will cut away, sand and polish you into a priceless jewel. Then watch your makeover transform you into a more effective personality for God's glory. Emulate the best of the rest and God will "finish" you better than you could ever imagine. Better yet, learn how Jesus adapted His personality in perfect ways and you will have a divine personality makeover.

Jesus' Personality

Obviously as humans, we are at a disadvantage. Jesus was divine, but He became human and was tempted in all the same ways we are (Heb. 4:15). In other words, He dealt with all the feelings we experience, but was able to overcome our natural bent to sin. Even though as God He could not err, He teaches us how each of the personality types can be both natural and divine. Consider these examples.

What was Jesus when He went in the Temple, cast out the money changers and overturned the tables (Mark 11:15)? Christ's obvious "D" behavior is seen as righteous indignation and was perfect for that time and place. He got mad, but He did not sin. There is a place for anger, but it must be controlled by the Holy Spirit.

What was Jesus when He preached to the multitudes in the open fields (Mark 1:22)? He told parables and stories that inspired and influenced people. He was a master communicator and charismatic leader. People were drawn to Him like "I" types, not just because of His personality, but because of the

Way, Truth, and Life (John 14:6). Never had anyone spoken like Him. Christ's persuasion was an example for every "I" type.

What was Jesus when He wept at Lazarus' tomb (John 11:35)? What personality did He exemplify when He was dying on the cross and told His disciple to take care of His mother (John 19:27)? Imagine that, Christ was suffering for the sins of the world and He was sensitive about His mother's welfare.

Jesus' "S" behavior is seen is so many ways — like a sheep being taken to the slaughter, He didn't resist or defend Himself (Isa. 53:7). He could have called 10,000 angels to wipe everyone off the face of the earth, but He was a gentle giant showing us how to win by losing. His meekness is still an example to every personality type.

What was Jesus when He went into the temple and taught truth people never heard before (John 7:14)? When He was just twelve years old, He dug into the marvelous mysteries of God. Christ's obvious "C" behavior is seen in His deep contemplation and knowledge. This may seem strange because He was God in the flesh, but He also had to learn in His humanity.

There are so many examples of Christ's exemplifying different personality types. The main lesson to learn is that He never mentioned that one personality is better than the other. He simply demonstrated how we should be "all things to all people." His "D" strength, combined with His "I" inspiration, and "S" sweetness, plus "C" carefulness is evident throughout the New Testament.

You, too, are a Living Epistle, known and read by everyone (2 Cor. 3:2). What message are people reading about your life? How balanced is your personality? How will your eulogy read when you die? Learn how to emulate all the good traits of all the personality types and you will develop a winning Christ-like personality.

5 *O*vercome your doubts and obstacles!

Moving out of their "comfort zones" can be very difficult to most people. "D" and "I" types may find it exciting, while "S"s and "C"s will be slower and more cautious to venture into an Extreme Personality Makeover.

"D" personalities are often like Captain Kirk of Star Trek going where no man has ever gone before. They like adventures and challenges. Taking risks is stimulating. Sometimes, they do not take the risks very seriously. "D"s need to be more careful.

"I" types also like to take chances, because they love the drama. They especially enjoy sharing the intrigue and story of how fascinating the experience was. They tend to be more optimistic. Their natural positive attitudes sometimes blinds them froms the potential problems. They, too, need to count the costs before proceeding.

"S"s struggle often with doubt and obstacles. They do not like new ventures or insecure situations. They tend to be stability-oriented. Their naturally steady and slow decisions make them safe adventurers. Once convinced to start, they are plodders, seldom quitting or disappointing others. If it gets too hard, they may reconsider, but in a relationship for the long haul.

"C" personalities are usually the most pessimistic and negative about challenges. They prefer investigating every possibility and considering all the facts before starting. They tend to be the last to venture our of their comfort zones, but once convinced it is the right thing to do, they usually end best. "C"s often finish their new ventures better than others, even when they are not first across the finish line.

The obstacles of life are varied, but often come from our

own self-doubt. Then there are also obstacles that others place before us. Finally, there are simple tests God allows to make us mature. Each of these obstacles will make us stronger or weaker. We will either wilt or win with our Extreme Personality Makeovers.

How we respond to the obstacles of life, will cause us to grow in God's grace or groan every time we think of what might have been. Our doubts, or the critical attitudes of others, will make us even more determined or will make us give up in the process.

For The Long Haul

Extreme Personality Makeovers involve long-term commitments. They are not quick-fixes or cute tricks we try to see if they work. Our makeovers will take months and maybe even years to unfold. Some people may notice changes right away, and others may not even realize what has happened until some time later.

The purpose is not to bring attention to ourselves, but to make us more effective and develop a winning Christ-like personality. The outcome should result in our glorifying God by being "all things to all people." Our makeovers should become transformations of our personalities into renewed ones that respond to the challenges of life as Christ would want us to.

The key to getting started is understanding what it will take to make us quit. Identifying and overcoming obstacles are imperative for a successful Extreme Personality Makeover. First, let us consider our self-doubt from a DISC perspective. Sometimes, we are our own worst enemies!

As optimistic as "D"s naturally can be, they may sabotage their progress by negative "self-talk." They usually do not attack themselves. They attack the process. In other words, they will

*O*vercome your doubts and obstacles!

ask themselves, "Is this absolutely necessary?" They often feel comfortable with who they are and to think they need to change is unnecessary.

"D"s expect everyone else to adapt to their demeanor. They often think everyone else is weak. Being self-assured is one of their trademarks. Their obstacle is often their confidence in the flesh. In other words, they can do whatever it takes with or without God.

Their mountain to climb will be their recognition of needing God and others to have a successful personality makeover. It will take a constant awareness of their wanting to be in charge or control. Letting go and letting others lead will be their biggest challenge at times.

Stumbling Blocks

"D"s will struggle more with stumbling over their own feet of forcefulness and failing to walk softly and slowly. They must guard against their strong desires to push forward no matter what. They will constantly need to be aware of the costs, consequences, and casualties while transforming into a gentle giant.

"I"s will hinder their climb to the top by not recognizing all those around them. There are those who also want to be at the top, plus there are those who do not care anything about being at the top. "I" types must control their drives and motivations to shine and look better than everyone else.

Rather than trying to "one up" others, by having a bigger and better fish story or exciting achievement experience, "I"s should allow others to stand out brighter than they. By recognizing their compulsion to talk, "I"s should control their tongues and let others share as long as they want.

Learn to ask questions, then pause and let others speak. "I" types sometimes try too hard to make everybody comfortable and have a good time. They often get too excited and expect everyone else to respond like they do. So "I"s get worse. They get louder and funnier, when they should be silent and give others time to reflect on the subject.

"I"s greatest obstacles are usually inflated by their egos. Their high opinion of themselves makes them too confident of their abilities. They often promise more than they can deliver. They should step back more and think before they promise.

Here is great advice for all "I"s when asked to do something: they should say, "Let me get back to you. I'd rather let you know than to let you down." "I"s often promise to do things and then forget about it or take on more than they can accomplish. Their reputation sometime becomes "braggers who do not deliver."

Guarding themselves from their well intended and often sincere desire to help is an obstacle to be reckoned with as soon as possible. Their obstacles often consist of sticking their foot in their mouth or stumbling over their own egos. Once "I"s learn to lift others above themselves and depend on the Lord to make them look good, there is no barrier that can stop their Extreme Personality Makeover.

Simple Things

"S"s stumble over the simple things, like "caring too much." How can anyone care too much? They often let people take advantage of them. But it usually does not bother them. They really do not care about themselves as much as they care about others. In fact, it makes "S"s feel great when they sacrifice themselves for others.

This seems odd, because everyone should become like "S"s. It is a wonderful trait they have, but overused it can become an abuse. They can become crippled by indecisions and letting others determine their every move. Even the very best thing about them can become something bad when they become their own obstacles.

"S" types must improve their self-images in ways that are different from what many people think of when improving themselves. "S"s often recognize they are good people, because they usually are better than most when you consider their kindness and caring. Their self-images need to improve in their self-doubt of thinking they can not do certain things, like speak publicly or take charge of a big challenge.

You can often hear "S"s saying to themselves, "I could never do that" or "I'm not qualified to take that on. Let someone else do it!" It is their lack of confidence that hinders their Extreme Personality Makeover. Yet "S"s are often the types who need it the most.

Self-Doubt

"C"s resist with self-doubt by reinforcing the negatives. They often build straw men, like Don Quixote, who is remembered best for fighting invisible foes. "C" types are great at finding the impossibility and then building their case for why things can not be done. As soon as they find a flaw or "fly in the ointment," they work from that obstacle and quickly come to the conclusion it is a waste of time.

Their strength of seeing things clearly and concisely often cripples them. The best thing about them is their ability to improve things, but disorganization and unclear plans often make it difficult for them to get pass the rhetoric or vision of others.

They would do better by seeing pass the problems and recognizing the goals as possibilities. "C"s initial responses are often red flags waving in the winds of change. They do not like change for change sake. They prefer improving and mastering things, but after much thought and preparation. "C"s need to become initiators of change from a positive perspective.

"C" personalities often need to become the cheerleaders and promoter-persuaders to try new things. They should change the self-talk to being more optimistic and excited about the possible results. Their obstacles need to be changed into opportunities.

Now let us consider the obstacles other people place in front of DISC types. These roadblocks are often the subliminal and quiet comments that affect us without our realizing them. Guarding against these influences will help us succeed in our Extreme Personality Makeovers.

"D"s Defense

For example, "D"s need to NOT let people tick them off. Instead of getting mad at someone who has wronged or threatened you, get even by controlling yourself. Recognize they win when they get under your skin and make you act unreasonably. The world, flesh, and devil work contrary to the Word of God. They often push you to do the opposite of what God wants.

There are times when you need to stand for something, but often your decision to do so is not always God's. People are often a pain, but how you respond to them can become even more painful. Simply weigh your tolerance to pain and decide which one is worth your endurance. The pain people often cause you must be countered with wiser decisions. Weigh the consequences and choose which pain you have to deal with that will bring about the best results.

The solution should always be based on which way you should go — the spiritual way of seeking peace and harmony or the natural (sinful) way of getting even or fighting to win at all cost. The choices for "D"s when others force an issue can be

*O*vercome your doubts and obstacles!

much harder when they decide to do what is right and not what is expedient or explosive.

"I"s Defense

"I"s also struggle with the obstacles others place before them. They often try to talk their way out or through the resistance. They are masters at manipulating people. "I" types are often the best at selling people things they do not need. They also turn the roadblocks around and create lemonade out of the sour lemons people throw at them.

They are proverbial optimists, but can get discouraged when people do not respond with the same enthusiasm. Recognizing their need for approval, "I"s should simply step back and pause in the conversation and find something they agree on. Do not let opposition cause emotional responses or irrational rhetoric that muddies the water.

"I"s should demonstrate strength when "D"s try to intimidate them. They should paint a win-win picture to follow "I"s. They must also seek clear thinking and rational logic as they deal with "C" types. Recognizing the potential deal-killers, "I"s should learn how to negotiate around negatives. This will help "I"s bypass the obstacles more easily and smoothly.

"S"s Defense

"S"s are especially vulnerable to obstacles because they are so naturally agreeable. Others find "S"s easy when it comes to changing their minds or actions. "S"s are often thought of as "Yes" types. They seldom resist the demands of a strong leader. "S"s make even better leaders than "D"s when they learn how to be as strong as "D"s while retaining the "S" traits.

"S"s strength is in their sweetness and softness, but the

obstacles other place in front of them are often hard and difficult things. "S"s therefore must prepare themselves for and expect these stumbling block to come their way. They should not be surprised at the rudeness of "D" and "C" types. "S"s should see it coming and defuse it with a strong comment like, "that was unnecessary. Aren't we both wanting the same thing — to win or — to correct the problem?"

This shows the "S"s ability to withstand force against them. They can also say to "I"s, "let me talk for a moment and please don't interrupt me. What you are about to learn can make you really look good."

"C"s Defense

"C"s tend to be generally critical thinkers. They will also express their displeasure with incompetence and incorrectness. Even when they do not express it verbally, they tend to demonstrate it with their attitudes and actions. An air of disgust can often be seen on their faces. Moodiness and melancholy feelings seem to engulf them when things do not go as planned.

They need to resist bad pessimism. Their natural ability to notice problems before others is a tremendous asset, but their displeasure often leads to disdain from those who are the target of correction. "C"s justify their actions with the defense that they are right about recognizing the problem. They should hold back from criticizing until they come up with several solutions.

Learning how to deal with the obstacles others place in our paths is vital to our Extreme Personality Makeover. We will either let people trip us "down" or we will turn their obstacles into stepping stones to climb over and pass the problems.

Obstacles can also be simple tests in life to make us more Christ-like. The main reason for having an Extreme Personality Makeover is to become more mature and effective as Christians.

*O*vercome your doubts and obstacles!

We should never fall into the trap of thinking we have "arrived" and there is no room for improvement. An honest evaluation of our strengths and "uniquenesses" will bring us back to reality. No one person or personality is an island or end to itself.

Everyone needs improvement; therefore, God allows trials and tests to coming into our lives as "life's lessons" to make us better. Some people handle tests by becoming bitter, rather than better. The choice is yours. You can let the challenges and disappointments of life turn you away from God's eternal plan for your life, or you can allow the test to draw you closer to where Christ is.

God allows crisis to always draw you closer to where Christ is. It is not just a play on words. It is also a powerful truth to live by. Every time a crisis knocks at your life's door, remember that you can allow it to enter as a friend or a foe. No one likes crisis that come at the worst times, but looking back we can often say those trials were the best things that ever happened to us.

Summary Thoughts

"D"s need to guard against going into immediate action and solving the problem. Sometimes a wait and see attitude is best. Also consider the Psalmist's "Selah!" — pause and consider. The best thing about "D"s is their ability to see what needs to be done and jump right into doing it. That is why they make great commanders and directors. But sometimes a slower and thoughtful approach will be better.

"I"s deal with the tests of life often more optimistically than others, but they can become hysterical with emotions. They make great actors and crisis often puts them on center stage. "I" types need to saturate their responses with doses of honesty and sincere emotions. Above all, they need to lift up Christ and point all the attention to Him, rather their troubles.

"S"s must allow their tests to become testimonies of God's strength and power to see them through. They often have the most potential to show God's grace, because people think of them as so "weak." They are actually the most meek and when troubles come they can demonstrate their strength in the midst of their weakness. Scripture reminds "S"s, "when I am weak, then am I strong."

"C"s can turn their tests into opportunities to teach others about God's reasonable and rational plan for their lives, even when the crisis makes no sense. "C"s' optimistic and faithful responses will speak louder than any sermon others will hear. When "C"s respond to trials without becoming moody or depressed, others will notice and ask how they can be so strong? These will be great chances for "C" types to teach people the unchanging truths of God's Word.

Right Perspective

The key to overcoming doubts and obstacles is recognizing how we tend to naturally respond and often do the exact opposite. When you find yourself getting down, remember you are seated with Christ in the heavenlies. Remember where you are seated, above principalities and powers. You are more than conquerors. There is no reason to look up when you are already up. Keep looking down!

Overcoming is often a matter of your perspective. Focus on Christ and allow Him to control your personality, rather than letting your personality control you. Become an overcomer by experiencing an Extreme Personality Makeover from a biblical perspective. Simply substitute your natural responses with God's supernatural power and watch what He will do through you!

6

*V*isualize what you can become!

Seeing the end results once you complete your Extreme Personality Makeover should really encourage you. Imagine if you are a "D" type, getting into a heated confrontation and not losing your cool. As an "I" personality, suppose you are surrounded by a group of people and you let others speak more than you. If you are a "S" type, imagine you are challenged by someone and you take a strong stand causing them to back down. And as a "C" type, think of a situation where you surprise everyone with an optimistic and enthusiastic response to someone else's proposal.

These are possibilities even without an Extreme Personality Makeover. If you are a mature Christian and have already graduated from the "School of Hard Knocks," you have probably already learned these lessons. But there seems to be areas we still need to improve. We often do not want to admit it, but we never "arrive" at the place where we can not learn more.

Our Personalities Often Betray Us!

Depending on how we tend to think, feel, and act, we visualize what we can become from a tainted perspective. "D"s often think they can become "King of the mountain," while "I"s envision themselves becoming "Superstars." The more humble "S"s are usually content just being someone's "significant other" or "faithful friend to the end." "C" types desire to be seen as competent and compliant team players who make a difference.

These evaluations are broad judgments open to varying degrees of differences depending on each person's maturity and blend of personality types and spiritual gifts. There are many factors that determine a person's true vision of what they can become. Many of these descriptions are generalities to be taken lightly. You, alone, will decide which ones are appropriate for you.

A lot of what you visualize concerning your potential will be based on your self-worth, regardless of your DISC personality type. If you are a "D" with low self-esteem, you may struggle more with control and anger. "I" types seem to seek more attention and need lots of approval. The more sweet and sensitive "S" personalities with poor self-images tend to withdraw further and feel even more inadequate. "C"s who do not think well of themselves are more introverted and worry more than most people.

Once you see your self-worth from a biblical perspective, you will recognize how special you are. God does not make any junk and you are seen by God as a precious and priceless jewel. You should not moan and groan in self-pity or doubt your worth, because you accept "it is He Who has made us!"

An Eternal Focus

Visualizing your potential in light of eternity should shed a whole new light on your well-being and attitude. Christians who wallow in the muck and mire of self-pity have not come to grips with God's declaration that they are His handiwork. God made no mistake in allowing them to become who they are today. But at the same time, "eye has not seen, nor ear heard, neither has it entered in the mind" of His children "the things God has prepared for them who love Him" (1 Cor. 2:9).

Focusing on what we can become must begin with a clear understanding of who and Whose we are. Then we can begin to build a better perspective of our future through an Extreme Personality Makeover. To help get a clearer picture, we should see

*V*isualize what you can become!

who we were before Christ, who we are now in Christ, and who we can become through Christ.

Remember Where You Came From

"D," "I," "S," and "C" types should remember what they were like before Christ came into their lives. Many believers came to know the Lord early in life and will not fully appreciate this part of the lesson. They are more fortunate than others who trusted Christ later in life, perhaps as teenagers or adults. The older you were when you came to Christ, the more you can understand the difference He has made in your life.

If your relationship with Him has grown cold, regardless of when you trusted in Him as your Savior, but you are now reconsidering your need for Him to be the Lord of your life, you will appreciate the difference He can make. Once you recognize He can run your life better than you can, it will be a great and glorious day for you. If He can forgive your sins and give you eternal life as a gift, He can take care of all your needs now.

One of your greatest needs here on earth will be solving your "people-problems." By visualizing and remembering what you were before Christ, you can begin to develop an awareness of what He wants you to become in regards to your personality. Each type has its specific challenges. As you review them individually, try to visualize how this affects what you can become.

"D"s before Christ were probably very confident and demanding types who did not care what anyone thought or felt. They considered themselves as "self-made" types standing on their own two feet. "D" types are sometimes very difficult to convert, because they tend to have the attitude that they do not need anyone. It usually takes a major encounter for them to humble themselves and admit they are in need of a Savior.

"D"s tend to be more cocky and self-sufficient. Before Christ, they probably struggled more with their aggressive and assertive personalities. Even after coming to the Lord, many "D"s bring that old nature and drive into their new Christian life. Even though "old things are passed away," the flesh continues to affect them under pressure. Even "D" type Christians who have known the Lord for a long time, can still struggle with anger-management.

"D"s' Turn Around

Once they trust the Lord, "D"s tend to be more sensitive to their outbursts and loss of control. The Holy Spirit continually convicts them of their weakness. As "D"s mature in Christ, they learn to calm down and be more gentle. There should be major differences in "D"s from before and after trusting Christ when it comes to overuses and abuses of their personalities.

If not, this Extreme Personality Makeover may be exactly what they need. If there is not a change in "D"s' temper and intimidating personality, they should reevaluate if they truly understood what it means to trust in Christ as their Savior. If they are depending on anything other than the finished work of Christ on the Cross, they should settle their eternal destiny once and for all. They should simply admit to God they need Him alone for salvation . . . that they can do nothing to add or take away from what Jesus did at Calvary . . . then put their complete faith in His death, burial, and resurrection alone to forgive them.

Once "D"s do this, they can know for certain they have eternal life. God will also put within them the power of the Holy Spirit to conquer their dependency on their self-will and way of life. God will break, mold, and make "D"s into new types who recognize the Lord as the Supreme Ruler of all their thoughts, feelings, and actions. They will no longer have to give in to

Visualize what you can become!

the temptation to get mad in order to get people to do what they think people ought to do.

Before Christ, "D"s could be arrogant and angry types. Once they trust Christ, they still become mad, but not sin by getting out of control. As they mature in the Lord, they grow to a place where they become as strong as steel and as soft as velvet. They learn to obey God by controlling themselves more than trying to control others. Their Extreme Personality Makeover through Christ transforms them into some of the most powerful leaders possible.

"I"s' Turn Around

"I"s, before trusting Christ, tended to be self-serving individuals who seemed to worship themselves more than God. "I" types were either loud-mouths or slick manipulators. Depending on their maturity as individuals without Christ, they could have been egotistical or really sharp and popular types who were well-liked by most people. Their approval and recognition could have made them proud in themselves.

Admitting they needed the Lord was difficult for them. Blinded by their good works or keen ability to hide their selfishness, "I"s could mask their need for anyone who could save them. They tended to be their own saviors. Their popularity would often overshadow their emptiness. Having many friends and so much fun filled their void as unbelievers.

Once Christ comes into their lives, "I"s tend to become the most excited and expressive types. Their personalities usually explode with joy realizing Christ has come to give them abundant, as well as eternal, life. "I"s tend to be the types who can not keep the good news to themselves. They often want to shout it from the mountain tops.

They tend to get "gloriously saved," if they come to Christ

after a life full of sin, greed and selfishness. "I"s are often the types who really appreciate the difference the Lord makes in the lives of those who not only get saved from sin, but also saved from self.

"I"s sometimes think they can trust Christ as their Savior and live as they please. They really do not understand how the same grace that paid for their sins will also discipline their way of life. God's plan is to save them from their guilt and themselves. The Lord wants to give them an Extreme Personality Makeover from the inside out. It is not enough to just act like a Christian. The Holy Spirit will chasten "I"s as God's children so they will follow Him in complete obedience.

Character vs. Reputation

"I"s tend to put on a good show when others are watching. They act superbly in front of the crowd, but often have secret sins they hold on to. God knows their hearts and will allow them to reap what they sow. Eventually the truth will be known about "I"s dedication to the Lord. Their true character will be revealed and their motives will become known. "I"s need to serve the Lord with gladness, but also honesty. They need to be just as pure in what they do on the inside as they tend to demonstrate on the outside.

Their Extreme Personality Makeover will be evident by their humility and quietness. It will be obvious when they learn to let others shine more than they, and when they let others out-talk them. Since "I"s seem to be so popular, the change will be evident when they pass the praise they deserve on to others. Their makeover will be one that lifts others above them — as they decrease, God increases in their lives.

*V*isualize what you can become!

"S"s' Turn Around

Lost "S"s without Christ often demonstrate Christ-like behavior, because they are so kind and nice to begin with. People seem to equate "S" demeanor with spirituality. Religious people are supposed to act like "S"s. The Beatitudes, also known as the "attitudes that ought to be us" include, "Blessed are the meek!" Being meek and mild are sure signs of "S" personalities. But it does not mean an "S" is a Christian.

In fact, it may be harder for "S"s to grasp the gospel, because they tend to be naturally good people. Convincing them of their sin and shortcoming can be difficult. As unbelievers they often "act" the act, "talk" the talk, and "walk" the walk. It is all useless, because everyone has to come to the place where they recognize that sin has separated them from Christ and all the good works in the world can not pay for their wrongdoing.

Prior to conversion, "S"s may have led exemplary lives, but they were powerless to save or change their destination or drives. They were motivated to be good people and no one else could do it better than "S"s. They often lived what some would think were good Christian lives, yet without the Lord. They could be like the Pharisees in Christ's day. They were often proud of their good deeds.

Before And After

Once they understand the good news that Jesus came to seek and to save that which was lost and they too needed a Savior, "S"s came quietly and humbly to the cross. Without fanfare or show, "S"s trusted Christ because they honestly recognized their shortcoming of the perfection needed to forgive their sins.

Upon trusting Christ, "S"s often become faithful servants. Sometimes there is not much noticeable change from before they made their conscious decision to believe in Christ as their only way to heaven. "S"s usually do not struggle a lot with doing good deeds. They wrestle more with "who" is going to do these deeds? Will it be Christ in them or will they continue just like before they trusted the Lord, as good people doing what needs to be done through their own human efforts?

Just like the other personality types, "S"s must realize they are powerless apart from Christ. Even though being good comes easy for them, good works neither save nor keep them. They must allow the Lord to do good works through them to honor and glorify God. This can be very confusing to "S"s because they were normally good before Christ came into their lives. Now, as Christians, they often find it difficult to stop being good through their human effort and allow God to be good through them.

You Will See A Change

Their Extreme Personality Makeover will be evident in the areas that were not natural for them before coming to Christ, and in the areas they have wrestled with throughout their lives. For example, "S"s tend to be quiet and shy. After their makeover, they should be more expressive in front of a crowd. They will also be more assertive and confident after their makeovers.

"S"s will seem more upbeat and enthusiastic. They will also demonstrate more analytical and reasoning behavior. It is not enough for "S"s to think they are ahead of everybody else because of their natural kindness and nice behavior. They may need to learn to be harder and stronger with others. Instead of letting people take advantage of them, their makeover will result in their turning the tables and showing people who is really in charge.

"S"s should constantly remember, "I can do all things

*V*isualize what you can become!

through Christ!" Their makeovers may seem more radical than the others, because they tend to be more laid back. Once "S"s master their makeovers, they will make great impressions on people. They will obviously be noticed because of their outgoing and friendly behavior. The once "wallflower" will have turned into a "social butterfly" and everyone will be amazed.

"C"s' Turn Around

"C"s tend to be the most doubting and questioning types before and after coming to Christ. Their endless inquires make them obvious skeptics. Before trusting Christ, they often contemplated the deepest questions of life. Their need to know why, what, how, and who made them serious investigators. Coming to Christ was usually not a leap into the dark. It was their most logical decision ever.

Some "C" types skip the scrutiny and rush into faith in Christ because they get tired of searching. They come to the end of their intellectual selves and recognize the solution is coming to trust the all-knowing One. Many "C"s who often ridiculed the faith, become believers even without the facts and evidence they naturally seek. They often come to a place where they can not find all the answers and finally take the plunge to trust Christ with simple child-like faith.

"C"s who experience this kind of beginning often make the best teachers. They do not need answers to everything. They learn early "faith comes by hearing and hearing comes by the Word" (Rom. 10:17). Their foundation is built on the Bible, not on the wisdom of this world or the ability to reason and convince people of the truth in Scriptures.

"C"s often struggled before Christ with simple platitudes and shallow answers for the reason of our faith. Once converted through the washing and regenerating power of the Word (Tit. 3:5), "C"s have a new mind and way of thinking. They may still want to dig deep into the Word, philosophy, and science, but the Spirit within brings them back to the Holy inspired Word of God.

Prior to an Extreme Personality Makeover, "C"s who know Christ as their Savior can still be boring and so deep that they put everyone to sleep. Once they recognize that their strengths of investigating and presenting the "deep things of the Word" often sabotaged their presentations, they can become exciting and influencing teachers.

Their Extreme Personality Makeover should create an atmosphere of exciting learning demonstrated by obvious body language and vivid stories that bring the lessons to the heart as well as the mind. No longer will "C"s be cold and staid. Their makeover should cause them to be active and expressive. Turning into actors and orators with gusto, they will capture the attention of audiences and amaze the greatest skeptics, because the "C"s substance was saturated with life-impacting style. People will be captivated not only by what is taught, but also by the teacher.

How Do You See Yourself?

Visualizing yourself before and after coming to know Christ can be practical, if you truly desire an Extreme Personality Makeover. The question now is, "Do you still see yourself as you were before Christ with all those rough edges or do see yourself as a new creation in Him?" Just as gemologists can take diamonds from the rough and cut and form them into beautiful jewels, so God wants to do the same for you.

Visualize yourself as a diamond in the rough. When God found you and when you found Him, God began to cut away

*V*isualize what you can become!

those rough spots forming you into a valuable person. He brought an Extreme Personality Makeover into your life, like gemologists polish and shine their diamonds into brilliant jewels.

God is recreating you in Christ so you can show His glory. He wants you to visualize your finished product and see what you can become when you simply let Him do it through you. He will be faithful and He WILL do it, if you just trust and obey Him.

Your challenge will be with the little letter "I." This is not referring to the "I" personality type. It is the "you" in you. The "I" in all of us will determine whether we allow God to have His way or our way in our lives.

The middle letter in the word "sin" is "i." Also one of the two middle letters in the word "Christ" is "i." Scripture admonishes us, "I can do all things through Christ," (Phil. 4:13). Notice this verse begins with "I" and ends with "Christ." Humanists and New Agers today start with "I" and end with "things." God desires that we start with the understanding that "I" am a sinner in need of Christ. Then we can move on to trust Him and learn how to do "all things through Christ Who strengths us."

Regardless, even if things seem to start or revolve around "I," they MUST end with Chr"i"st in us, the hope of glory. "For me to live is Christ and to die is gain," (Phil. 1:21).

It is okay to improve yourself, but it should always be done with eternity's values in view. Christians should seek to be the most effective people in the world for God's glory. We should visualize ourselves as Ambassadors for Christ (2 Cor. 5:20), representing the King of Kings. Everything we say and do should show our faith and good works as we become what He would have us be.

*E*xercise each personality type to improve!

Putting your Extreme Personality Makeover into action will require strenuous exercises. You will have to control your strengths by not overusing them. Identifying your weaknesses are also important. Everyone will have to work on exercising each of the personality types in order to have a successful makeover.

No one is exempt or can skip this lesson, because everyone has specific needs to improve or control themselves. For example, "D"s may think they do not need to enhance their task skills, because they are already masters at multi-tasking. Their need is to avoid taking on too many projects. They also tend to sacrifice family needs and spend too much time on their work responsibilities. They often become "workaholics" and sometimes need interventions to change these shortcomings.

"I"s may think they do not need to improve their people skills, because they are so well-liked and comfortable with crowds. They often need to exercise restraint in conversations. Talking too much is just as much a fault as not speaking at all. Disciplining their drives to express themselves can be extremely difficult for "I" types.

"S"s can fall into the trap of thinking they are so kind and nice that they do not need to improve in those areas. They can be faithful to a fault. In other words, they can be so tolerant and forgiving that people abuse or use them. "S" personalities may need to exercise their emotional muscles to be stronger and forceful with others.

"C"s may rationalize they are the wisest and most intuitive when it comes to problem solving. This may be true, but they can also be the slowest or most difficult types at the same time. Their drive to do things perfectly sometimes causes them to waste time on unnecessary details. They can also become moody and worry too much. "C"s may need to exercise more positive mental attitudes and optimistic thinking.

To improve, let us take a closer look at exercising all the personality types from spiritual, mental, emotional, and physical perspectives.

Exercising Your Personality From A *Spiritual* Perspective

"D"s should constantly exercise spiritual habits, such as prayer, Bible study, fellowship, worship, and sharing their faith. "D" types can get so caught up in "other" things they set aside godly duties. To succeed in their Extreme Personality Makeovers, they will have to exercise their spiritual needs as well as spend time on the multitude of other tasks.

To make this exercise simple and practical, schedule your daily quiet time and devotions with God like you do your daily schedule. Prioritize time for God. Pray daily that God will control your drives. Think past the present when things get heated and ask God to guard your assertiveness and actions. Above all, let the Lord be the master of your fate and captain of your ship.

"I"s should also set aside time every day to fellowship and speak with God. They tend to get sidctracked and bypass their time for God. A telephone call will interrupt their devotions and "I"s will often spend more time on the phone with a friend than they will with God and His Word. Whatever type you are, do not let anything come between you and God. He is your best friend.

*E*xercise each personality type to improve!

Let Him speak to you through His Word and talk to Him more than you talk to everyone else about your problems.

Also, exercise the principle of passing on the praise you receive. Be more conscious of when people praise you. Do not absorb the compliments and seek more pats on the back. Wait for a pause in the conversation, then sincerely pass the praise on to the Lord. Always remember, He gave you every good thing about you and He will not share His glory with anyone.

"S"s should exercise their need for security and stability from a spiritual perspective by resting in God's Word and His Holy Spirit within them. It will be difficult at first, but once "S"s trust and obey what God tells them to do in the Scriptures, they will increase their faith to do even more than they ever thought they could do.

"S" types should have daily exercises where they spend time with God, then go through the day depending on Him so they can do all things through Christ. This exercise will often develop the areas that may seem weak on the outside, rather than the inside. "S"s tend to be strong within, but may need to be stronger outwardly to show their faith, not only by their works, but also by their words.

Exercising Your Spiritual Muscles

"C" personalities should exercise their spiritual muscles by studying the Holy Scriptures for a sweeter relationship with God, as opposed to digging into the Word to discover deeper truths. "C"s tend to be great students, but Jesus also wants to have an intimate, as well as an intellectual, relationship with them. Studying the Word and gaining more knowledge is good, but finding the precious passages that speak to "C"s' hearts, as well as their minds, are vital exercises.

"C" types are often more concerned with winning an argument than winning the soul to Christ. They should exercise more tenderness and timing as they seek to be more spiritually led in all they do. Getting the job done perfectly is sometimes not as important as building spiritual relationships with others.

Exercising all the personality types from a spiritual perspective is so important, but strengthening our personalities from a mental and emotional perspective is also vital.

Exercising Your Personality From An *Emotional* Perspective

"D" personalities can be intense or very quiet. They sometimes give the first impression of being "S" types. Often giving mixed signals, they can be hard to read. Their emotions tend to be more serious and "bottom line" than others. They often need to exercise more patience. Their motivation to get the job done "now" often bothers people.

Exercising restraint is most important for "D"s. Learning how to control their emotions, rather than letting their emotions control them, will make the difference in the success or failure of their makeovers. Like the "Incredible Hulk," "D" types need an antidote to calm their emotions, so their actions will not be destructive. Their determination to control themselves must be stronger than their obsessions and emotions to control others.

"I"s do not have to exercise their emotions from an active perspective. They need to discipline their feelings to be more passive than active. Instead of responding in obvious ways, "I"s should learn to be more still and quiet. It is common for "I" types to get excited and share their feelings.

It is uncommon for "I"s to be reserved and calm. This seems so unnatural, but it can be the more mature and spiritual behav-

*E*xercise each personality type to improve!

ior. "I" personalities must focus on being what God wants them to be, rather than wanting to be themselves. The idea of being "real" has been distorted to the place where people have the right to be crazy and dysfunctional because that is just the way they are. "I"s will improve their effectiveness as they learn balance in their emotional lives.

"S"s are more passive and slower emotionally to respond. Their challenges will often be NOT responding sooner, or NOT even responding at all. They tend to back off and wait to see what will happen first. "S"s are the best at leaving conflicts alone and thinking hopefully that they will go away. Exercising their responsiveness to act sooner and stronger is often more important.

Fight Or Flight

"S"s should consciously notice when they want to back away and withdraw. They should resist their natural tendencies and prayerfully respond with confidence. They sometimes even need to fight, rather than flee. They should exercise their wills to avoid becoming doormats. They should become driving forces for the good things they sincerely want to see accomplished.

"C" personalities need to exercise more emotional responses, because they tend to be so unemotional. It is usually difficult for them to show initial love and care, but that does not mean they are incapable of having these emotions. "C"s just do not exhibit their emotions as openly as other types. Therefore, they need to work on outwardly demonstrating the same feelings they may have on the inside for someone or a particular project.

Exercising and strengthening "C"s emotional awareness will involve special efforts, because it usually does not come naturally. They may have to force themselves to feel for others. Getting pass the "fake" and "falseness" of their showing deep feelings, when those emotions are not strong, is almost impossible for "C"s. They often pride themselves as being "real" and honest about everything. Learning how to care and confront with love will greatly improve their personality makeover.

Exercising Your Personality From A *Mental* Perspective

Scripture teaches, "As a man thinks, so is he" (Prov. 23:7). Your mind is the thinking part of your brain. Your brain is a phenomenal organ designed to do millions of things without you thinking about them. It is automatic. You do not have to make any decision. Your brain does what it was divinely designed to do all by itself.

On the other hand, your mind is the part of your brain that is controlled by the choices you make. In other words, the brain is "programmed" to keep your heart beating even when you sleep. Your brain takes care of all your subconscious body functions. Your mind, on the other hand, is influenced by how you think, feel, and act. Your personality has a lot to do with stimulating your mind.

The decisions you make throughout each day will strengthen or weaken your mind's ability to help or hurt you. When you put garbage into your mind in the form of wrong thinking, you will suffer. Ironically, there is a place for cautious and careful pessimistic thinking, but it should not control you. There is a place for negative thinking, but you should only be negative about the things God's Word warns.

To be constantly pessimistic or to be overly optimistic can warp your mind into "stinkin' thinkin'." You must train your mind to think as God would have you. Disciplining and filtering

*E*xercise each personality type to improve!

what comes into your mind is so important.

"D"s' Mental Goals

"D" personalities should guard against being influenced by other "D" types who seem to have an aversion to fighting issues and philosophies. A constant diet of "D"s' rantings and ravings can create monsters. Being attracted to those who seem to be the only ones standing for the truth can be dangerous. On the other hand, God uses "D"s in great ways. Martin Luther took a stand on "the just shall live by faith" (Gal. 3:11) and sparked the Reformation. "D"s are often blessed by God to be "change agents," but need to be often reminded there is a big difference between contending for the faith and being contentious.

If you are a "D" type, watch and learn from all the other types, especially "S"s, to improve your effectiveness. Strengthen your mind with the enthusiasm of "I" types. Exercise your thinking to be more positive and pleasing as you challenge people. Also observe how "S"s tend to be so agreeable and kind. "D"s should also exercise their mind to think more analytically, rather than action-oriented like "C"s.

"I"s' Mental Goals

If you are an "I" type, fill your mind with thoughts of being more firm like "D"s. Weigh the consequences and lean toward being stronger, rather than popular. Also train your mind to notice how often you interrupt people.

Watch how "S"s show sincere attention and listen more than they speak. Guard your mind against looking around to see who is there. Continually smile, look directly into people's eyes and show sincere interest.

To exercise "C" behavior, take more time to prepare and organize your work. Condition your mind to plan your work and work your plan. Do more research and think thoroughly through things.

"S"s' Mental Goals

If you are a "S" type, exercise and strengthen your mind with active personality traits. Practice being more assertive and expressive. Work on responding, rather than withdrawing in a crowd. Speak up and out. Let people see your enthusiasm. Make a conscious effort to be more outgoing.

Notice how "D"s are confident. Observe "I"s' influencing styles. Heed how "C"s strategically tackle tasks with or without others helping. Exercise your mental being to make each type wiser.

"C"s' Mental Goals

If you are a "C" type, practice making decisions faster. Do not table everything for further review. Be more risk-taking. Respond with more "I" type positive attitudes, rather than doubting or looking for the flaws.

To think more like "I" types, forget about your inhibitions and let your hair down. Act a little crazy. People will notice and begin thinking you are not as serious as you usually are. Do not go overboard and do stupid things. Above all, change your thinking that everything has to be perfect before you will be satisfied.

Changing the way you think to emulate and act like other personality types will greatly enhance your effectiveness. Do not find fault with this advice and short-circuit the power God has given your mind. It is a marvelous part of your being that takes the decisions you make and allows you to enjoy life as God

*E*xercise each personality type to improve!

intended.

Make the wise decision to adapt your thinking as "D," "I," "S," and "C" types to become more Christ-like. Fill your mind with biblical thoughts and you will become all God would have you to be.

Exercising Your Personality From A *Physical* Perspective

When we consider how personality types affect our physical life, we must look at our actions. There are distinct ways each "D," "I," "S," and "C" type tends to respond from a physical perspective. We may feel strange dealing with how we are to move or be individually, but it might be something we may want to work on to improve our effectiveness.

Body language and non-verbal communication say a lot about us. We tend to communicate our feelings and thoughts through our actions. Exercising and practicing our actions to show all the personality traits is very practical. For instance, when speaking to "I" types it is so important to show excitement; while listening to "C"s we should show deep thought.

This may seem a little far-fetched, but there are legitimate reasons to improve our physical actions when relating to others. Sometimes, the way we say things are just as important as what we say. Notice the distinct body language of specific personality types and learn from their example. See if you can pick up little gestures and expressions each type exemplifies.

This may apply to the Apostle Paul's admonition "to the weak, I became weak and to the strong, I became strong" (1 Cor. 9:22). We can improve our relationships and effectiveness when we start exercising our outward actions to be more like the other personality types. These are the most difficult exercises to describe, but they may be some of the most practical to consider.

If you are a "D" type, guard against showing anger or intensity on your face. Be more open with your hands and arms. Instead of pointing your fingers at someone, use an open hand. Instead of banging your fist on a table or shaking your hand at someone, open your arms in a hugging-like gesture.

"I" types should exercise restraint with their body language. They often over react with their hands and facial expressions. This is good when speaking to other "I"s, but when communicating with other types it can take away from what you are saying. People often notice the gestures more than the message.

"S"s often need to be more expressive and active physically when they speak to others. Some nationalities, for example, Latin types, are more exuberant. They often speak with their hands. Yet, "S" types, regardless of their natural bent, seem to be more still and reserved with their bodies. They should exercise more movement and visual responses.

"C" types seem to give suspicious looks. They often appear like they are in deep thought. Sometimes people think "C"s are mad at them, when "C"s are just thinking deeply about something. "C"s should constantly be aware of the people around them and acknowledge their presence often. They should let people know they care more about them than whatever they are working on by saying "hello" or asking how they are.

Exercising our personalities from a spiritual, emotional, mental, and physical perspective is so important. It will not come naturally. The usual way we respond is from the way we were wired. It is not always the best way, because our flesh often interferes. Our ideal thoughts, feelings, and actions will be supernatural. We should think past the present and identify with those to whom we are relating. Adapting to their needs and interest is usually best.

8

*R*enew your commitment to adapt daily!

Time has different seasons, like life often has its cycles. Spring follows Winter. Budding trees and flowers spring from the deadness of Winter. So it is in our spiritual lives, when we die to our self-centeredness. Renewing our commitment to follow Christ is like Winter giving way to Spring. When Jesus died and was buried, everything looked bleak. After His death came the resurrection. We, as Christians, must also renew ourselves daily with resurrection life to follow Christ.

The key to a successful Extreme Personality Makeover is living the resurrected life of Christ. Anyone can take the principles laid out in this book and improve his or her effectiveness. It is a science that works for believers and unbelievers. Science is no respecter of persons. It works for and against everyone, regardless what they believe.

Renewal Is A Biblical Truth!

True renewal only works in those who have the Spirit of God within. Christians often grow cold and distant from each other and God. When couples and families understand the truth that Jesus is the vine and believers are the branches, then they can begin to renew their hearts and minds for a lasting personality makeover.

Having an Extreme Personality Makeover should be a continual process. It should not be a passing fancy or fad. It must take root and spring forth always growing toward maturity.

Those who simply read these principles and do not apply what they learn to their every day experiences will be like people who look in a mirror and do nothing about the problems they see.

Hopefully, you have experienced a look in the mirror. You should now take what you have learned and put it into practice. Just like the seasons of life, you must seek the natural and supernatural blessings that result from obeying God's laws. Doing what Human Behavior Science and the Bible tell you should follow what you have learned.

To Everything There Is A Season!

It is now time to blossom from the normal to the spiritual . . . from defeat to victory . . . from testings to testimonies of God's power in your life. It is now the season to live like you have never lived before. Breathe in the fresh air of God's Word and breathe out a renewed way of thinking, feeling, and acting.

Renew your commitment daily to adapt and become what God originally intended your personality to be in Him. Learn how to breathe in His truth and then release what you have received. Inhaling and exhaling His will and way through your specific personality requires that you renew your commitment every time your personality is stretched to be something it is not, but should be.

Each personality type seems to respond specifically to the need for renewal. "D"s tend to resist but they are broken and crushed through failures and disastrous experiences. "I"s are often open to renewal, but hesitate if it will cramp their free and casual lifestyles. "S"s are concerned about how renewal may threaten their families and comfort zones. "C"s tend to investigate what renewal involves and doubt its potential to improve the status quo.

Renew your commitment to adapt daily!

Simply trust God to finish His work in you. Let Him control your personality, instead of allowing your personality to control you. Come to a place where you release your will, mind, and feelings to God. He will share His overcoming power and way to victory with you. Then you will be able to share His truths with others. Sharing is God's way of blessing you. All that is His can belong to you if you learn the principle of "Sharing."

S-H-A-R-E

Each letter has a tremendous lesson for you to learn as you share with others.

"S" is for "Spiritual Gifts." Believers in Christ not only have personalities, but we have been endowed with spiritual motivations that also affect the way we think, feel, and act.

"H" stands for "Heart," our passions in life. Our hearts and passions also drive us to do what we do.

"A" is for "Abilities" and how God has blessed us with specific abilities to serve Him.

"R" can represent our "Renewed Personalities." Identifying and exercising our personalities is not enough. We need to "renew" our personalities to be what God wants.

"E" is for "Experience." Our lifetime of experiences can be turned into valuable service for God. He has been molding and making us to bless everyone as we "share" Him with others.

The main lesson is not what we get from God, but what we give back to Him and others. Getting is usually easier than giving. Keeping is often more difficult than sharing. Everything we gain from God, we must share with others. If not, the Law of Entropy will destroy all we have gained.

Having received from God our unique and special personality type means we need to give it back to Him. As we obey and serve Him through our motivations and drives, we become the person and personality He wants us to be. It is in the sharing that we gain back more than we had. When we adapt and give our personalities back to people the way they need us to, we receive more of what our personality was meant to be.

Sharing is the key to victory. Having a "Renewed Personality" will result in God finishing His work in our lives. We must stop holding on to the "that's just the way I am" attitude and begin sharing with others what they need from us. We then become what they require, plus God gives us back more than we gave.

All personality types tend to deal with sharing in their own ways. They resist and surrender differently. The lesson is not whether we get anything out of our Extreme Personality Makeover. The instruction is learning to share with others and help them. As we become "examples of the believers" (1 Tim. 4:12) by sharing, we will in return, "receive exceedingly abundant above all that we ask or think" (Eph. 3:20).

To renew their commitments and share what they have learned, each personality type has specific challenges and promises.

"D" Commitments

"D"s will often have to deal with becoming too busy for God. Even in ministry, they sometimes get caught up in the "work of the Lord" and forget about "the Lord of the work." "D"s must commit themselves daily by the renewing of their minds so they can discover what is that good and perfect will of God (Rom. 12:1,2).

"D" types must breathe in God's Word, pray, fellowship with other Christians, worship, and share the gospel if they are going to obey God. They will then have more power to "fight the good fight of faith." Through their letting God share His overcom-

*R*enew your commitment to adapt daily!

ing strength with them, they will then have the capacity to share what they have learned with others. When "D"s learn to be good losers, they really win. They can then share their true power with others, who in turn will share with others, who will in turn — etc. That is multiplying your losses into winnings. It is a paradox the natural mind can not understand.

This is a difficult concept to see, but "D"s usually understand exactly what it means to spiritually win by losing. Receiving by sharing does not make human sense, but it is a biblical principle that has worked since the beginning of time.

God shared His creation with humankind for us to give back to Him and others. If we hoard and keep it to ourselves, "getting all we can, canning all we get, closing the lid and poisoning the rest," will destroy what we conceal for ourselves.

Sharing our faith, possessions, and personalities with others by giving and being what they need will come back to bless us. We should not just give to get. That is also dangerous. We should share whether we get anything in return. True love gives without expecting anything in return. "D" personalities should give unconditionally without wavering or strings attached. They cannot intimidate God! They also cannot out give God.

"I" Commitments

"I"s, on the other hand, sometimes act as though they can manipulate God. He knows their hearts. The Lord knows if they have sincere motives. Sharing to be seen and applauded by others are abominations to God. He sees right through "I"s whose hearts are far from Him. Renewing their personalities to be selfless and sacrificing the recognition they deserve in order to praise others pleases God.

"I" types seem to receive more attention, especially when it comes to personalities, than all the others put together. Therefore "I"s have greater responsibilities to share what they receive. Scripture teaches those who receive more are expected to give more in return. "To whom much is given, much is required," (Luke 12:48). This may seem unfair, but many people feel "I"s seem to hog all the attention and steal the show. Some people even resent "I"s for standing out so much.

Therefore, "I"s must guard against absorbing all the glory they receive and humbly pass on the praise to those around them. Sharing for "I" types is very difficult. It can be seen especially when they were younger. As children, they often wanted to be in front of the crowd or camera. Jumping up so everyone could see them or making funny faces was what they were known for.

"I"s Love Attention!

As mature Christians with an Extreme Personality Makeover, "I"s will often do the opposite of what they feel like doing. They should quietly allow others to be lifted up above them. Sharing the "limelight" so others are praised more will be a great challenge to "I"s. Letting another person's lips praise them (Prov. 27:2) is strongly recommended if "I"s sincerely want to be what God would have them to be.

Sharing in conversations by allowing others to have equal time will test their makeover results. They should ask more questions and let people completely answer them without interruptions. When "I"s learn how to share all their great traits with others, it will make them look even better.

Actually, looking better should never be "I"s' motivations. "Being" better should be their goal. When they ARE better, people will notice. "Being" is much more important than "doing." "I"s can do the things they should with wrong motives.

Renew your commitment to adapt daily!

Once they become the person they should be, they will do the right things. That is why sharing is imperative to "I" types. As they share with others the praise that is rightfully theirs, then God blesses them even more.

The issue with most "I"s is learning to live the Crucified Life. It is "not 'I' who lives, but Christ in me, and the life I now live in the flesh, I live by the faith of the Son of God" (Gal. 2:20). Living the Resurrected Life is having a "Renewed Personality" that glorifies God, not self.

"S" Commitments

"S"s experience renewed personalities when they become stronger in the areas where they are weakest. To some people, "S"s' weaknesses are their strengths. In other words, their kindness and sweetness are not weaknesses. They are actually strengths. Simply put, their weaknesses are their "uniquenesses." The problem arises when "S"s allow people to take advantage of their kindness and are intimidated or manipulated to do things they should not.

Their renewed personalities will learn to be "weak to the weak and strong to the strong." The question here is whether "S"s will have the determination to do both parts. Being "weak to the weak" comes easy. Realistically, the answer is not in whether "S"s will do that part, but whether "S"s will let God do the "strong to the strong" part through them. "I can do ALL things through Christ Who strengthens me" (Phil. 4:13) is not a mantra to mumble, but a mandate for "S"s to obey.

"D"s must practice "S" behavior, while "S"s should exercise "D" traits. Every personality type should learn from the others. "S"s often must become like "I"s to influence and impress others with their communication skills. Ironically, "S"s can become accomplished actors and actresses. Away from the camera, "S"s may be shy and reserved, but in their thespian roles, they can act out opposite personalities. This is a great lesson for "S"s to understand. They may feel shy inside, but to do what needs to be done as "performers," they must become another person.

This may sound wrong to do, but every believer has been bought with a price (1 Cor. 6:19). They do not belong to themselves. They belong to God. They are, therefore, to "act" as God would have them. Their extroverted or introverted personalities are now God's. He is the "Director" and every personality type is at His command. When God yells, "lights, action, camera" we should take on the personality He would have us become.

As believers we are commanded to "become all things to all people" (1 Cor, 9:22). The world's way of thinking is going to criticize this teaching, because it does not understand the Christ-centered life. The whole "Me" generation" today is into self-gratification and self-elevation. The "Jesus First" generation is committed to renewing their personalities to become all things to all people and glorify God.

"C" types should contemplate the consequences of not renewing their personalities. What are their options? What do they have to lose? What if this is the way to victory, plus more effective living and ministry? Will you respond like wise "D"s and go for it? Will you get excited like "I"s? Will you learn from "S"s to be nicer and not so critical? You can answer those questions right now by honestly reflecting on how you are feeling about those personal inquiries.

Are You Mad?

Are you a little irritated by the insinuation that you are the type of person who would get upset? If so, that is exactly what

*R*enew your commitment to adapt daily!

this is all about. Step back and analyze how accurate this is. You have predictable patterns of behavior and you may have just betrayed yourself. You became your own critic. You judged yourself and were found guilty. Do not condemn the science. Learn from it and renew your personality to not respond so negatively.

If you accepted the previous questions with a spirit of optimism and the positive attitude that you have more to learn, then you are in the best position to renew your personality for God's glory. You are to be commended for thinking all this through and coming to constructive conclusions that will help you create practical application from your investigation.

Always Remember, Personality Profiling Is Just A Tool!

It is not a way of life or philosophy to judge people apart from the Scriptures. The Bible has nothing or little to say about personality types. There are only examples. Learn from those individuals in Scriptures that exemplified all different personality types. God does not care what your personalities are as much as He cares who is in control of your personalities.

Does it not make sense that God has the answers to everything and that you should obey Him even when you do not have the solution. Stop trying to figure everything out. "Faith is the substance of things hoped and evidence of things not seen," (Heb. 11:1). Practice stretching your faith. Trust God and others to move forward even when you are doubtful. Be a contagious optimist through the power of God to move mountains.

"C"s should use their competence and compliant personalities to influence more people through enthusiastic teaching. Next time you give a presentation or facilitate a class, get excited and share your depth of information like it is the most fascinating information you have ever learned. Add sparks, sugar and spice to your speech. Combine colorful style with your substance and watch how people respond better.

Regardless of what our "D," "I," "S," or "C" type is, we should renew our personalities daily. We can easily do this as we acknowledge Who is the source of our strength. The secret of success will be determined by Who is in control of our personalities.

Trials and troubles will come when we forget or, outright, NOT let Christ be the Lord of our personalities. When we violate God's natural and supernatural laws, plus try to run our own lives, we will fail. When that happens, we need to remember the "SOS" of life is our "Source Of Strength." God will then be our "Secret Of Success."

Renewing our personalities involves committing ourselves to the Lord daily. Success comes from "yieldedness." Scripture admonishes, "don't you know to whom you yield yourself to obey that servant you are" (Rom. 6:16)? This means we should "yield" ourselves to God as spiritual slaves. He, in turns, frees us as bond-servants (forgiven and released slaves) to serve Him willingly, not to pay back a debt, but to serve Him freely out of gratitude.

Yielding involves letting God live His resurrected life through us. When we want to act, think, or feel a certain way, we should stop and decide what Jesus would have us do. He will always desire we respond spiritually, rather than naturally. God may lead us to be exactly how He wired us through our predominate personality type. Yet sometimes, God wants us to respond the exact opposite way as a totally different personality type. Regardless, His Holy Spirit will guide us as we trust and follow His leading through His Word and witnesses (others).

*R*enew your commitment to adapt daily!

In Conclusion

The Bible commands, "don't be drunk with wine, but be filled with the Spirit" (Eph. 5:18). This verse primarily illustrates the need to be controlled by God, in the same way alcohol controls people. Alcohol often kills our inhibitions, fears, and typical way of responding.

People who are normally quiet and shy, can become loud and funny when under the influence of alcohol. People who are controlling and aggressive can become kind and nice. Unfortunately, drunk "D"s often become even more combative and obnoxious. The point is alcohol has an affect on people. God desires the Holy Spirit to also influence us to often be something we are not, in a good and perfect way.

When the stresses of life push and poke at you to turn you into monsters or mice, or to fight or flee, think about how the Holy Spirit wants to control you. He will help you make the wisest and best decisions. Your renewed personality will then demonstrate an Extreme Personality Makeover with superb results and effectiveness.

One Final Question

The final question is, will you yield to God's desire to use you how He knows is best or will you go your own way disregarding His will for your life? It is your choice. You will choose abundant life in Christ (John 10:10), which is greater than you can ever imagine, or will you live a so-called "normal" and mundane existence?

Choose His life and you are also guaranteed the stability and security His way provides, or you can take your chances on protecting yourself apart from God's promises. You can continue trying to figure all this out and boggle your brain with endless debate, or have the mind of Christ to answer all your questions.

You are now invited to a "coming out party." Get up from reading this book as a renewed personality. Live in the liberating power of God's promise to be conformed into His image (Rom. 8:29). The lie of Satan in the Garden of Eden was to make Adam and Eve like "little gods" for their own self-pleasure and eventual destruction. Today's philosophy poisons people to think they are their own gods. Many people believe they are gods unto themselves. This is a tragic error to believe.

On the other hand, Jesus invites you to come unto Him, if you labor and are heavy laden (Matt. 11:28). If the burdens of broken relationships and the pain of strife seem to be heavier than you can carry, Jesus will give you rest.

Just like a yoke or harness that goes over the head of oxen for pulling and plowing purposes often has two places for the beasts of burdens to place their heads through, Jesus will come along side you and place His head in your yoke to pull you out of the burdens of life.

In other words, if you take His yoke of liberty and power on you, He will do all the pulling. His burden is easy and His yoke is light, because He will do His work through you. Just let Him! He will not make you do the right things. You must decide to do His will not yours. The Lord is waiting on you to let go and let Him has His way in your life. He can make your Extreme Personality Makeover the miracle some people think will never happen with your type.

Now, enjoy your makeover and share it with others!

Postscript

Having an Extreme Personality Makeover is just the beginning of your "makeover miracle" journey! Once you trust Christ as your Savior, God begins a process in you that will affect every area of your being. He first comes into your life as an invited "guest." He Who created the universe will not be content just being a guest in your life. He desires to become the "host" of your home and begins rearranging the furniture — your possessions and habits. Finally the Master Builder of our lives will not be finished with you until He becomes the "Head" and the very essence of your existence.

From being just an invited guest to becoming the Head of your life, Jesus stands ready to finish His work in you. You can continue to resist and suffer the consequences of a rebellious life, but be advised, "for whom the Lord loves, He chastens and scourges every son and daughter He receives (Heb. 12:6). God definitely deals with His disobedient children. Don't be deceived, whatever you sow, you will also reap (Gal. 6:7). If you sow your wild oats, you will reap the whirlwind.

Investing In Your Life

Plant good seeds and watch God grow a harvest of blessings in your life. Continue your maturing process and look for other areas to improve your makeover. Begin thinking about an Extreme "Wellness" Makeover! Examine your physical health, as well as your spiritual wellness. Be just as committed to glorifying God with your body as you are with your soul and spirit.

Our personalities have a lot to do with our motivations. These drives also affect our wellness. Begin praying that God will help you improve your health for His glory and your benefit.

If you neglect your wellness, your health will become an enemy. People often spend all their health to get their wealth, then have to spend all the wealth to get their health back.

Our next Extreme Makeover book is going to focus on Health and Wellness from a biblical perspective. Many people need to learn how to have an extreme encounter with the creator of their bodies in order to improve the physical care they need. Sometimes it seems we do not really care about ourselves or we ignore God's admonitions about glorifying Him with our "body and spirits" (1 Cor. 6:19-20).

To become the Christians we should be, we need to obey the whole counsel of God (Acts 20:27). We should follow all the Scriptures which also teach us about taking care of our bodies. Start now by praying God will reveal the habits that hurt your body. Be sensitive to the Holy Spirit's leading and listen closer to those who teach about physical, as well as, spiritual health.

Learning More

We are also considering a series of "Extreme Makeover" books and we would greatly appreciate your thoughts. Let us know if there is a specific subject you would like us to investigate. Email Dr. Carbonell at: drmels@myuy.com or phone: (706) 492-5490. Also take advantage of other Uniquely You Resources. Go to our web site at: ***www.myuy.com*** and click on ***Products*** to review the various profiles and resources available.

If you are interested in becoming a "Certified" consultant, coach or trainer, review our ***Training*** information. Helping people improve their quality of life and relationships with others are so rewarding. Seriously consider leading a group in your church or organization through an ***Extreme Personality Makeover*** course.

You may also want to become one of our Masters Institute trainers to facilitate individuals and / or groups in the process of having an Extreme Personality Makeover. The opportunities are endless and can be so rewarding. Consulting and coaching are some of the fastest growing industries available to anyone today.

One of the best things you can do is encourage others to complete an *Extreme Personality Makeover Profile* over the internet. The online *EPM Profile* will offer a DISC *Uniquely You Questionnaire*, plus all the information in this book. People can complete their profiles at their convenience any time 24/7.

The results of their assessment will be electronically plotted on two graphs revealing their DISC "Behavior Expected By Others" (response to their environments) and their "Instinctive Response To Pressure" (the "Real You") from a DISC perspective. Receive an instant report with the same insights in this book, then apply the personalized information to improve relationships and effectiveness.

To complete an *EPM Profile* with an online questionnaire and report, go to: ***www.UniquelyYou.Net*** then click on ***Extreme Personality Makeover.***

People can also purchase this book from our web site as a pdf text to download. Send it to a friend, relative or associate. To purchase the online version of the book with a ***FREE*** code ($35 value), go to ***www.UniquelyYou.com*** then click on ***Products***. The online report, just like this book, is all about helping improve relationships with God and others. We deeply want to help people *do* and *be* all that God wants.

Let us know how we can help. May God bless you while you mature through your makeover to become more like the Master!

Your Human Resources Center

Uniquely You is a Christ-centered, Bible-based ministry dedicated to empowering and equipping Christians through discovering their giftedness. Uniquely You specializes in the Science of Human Behavior from a biblical perspective. Results-oriented training and proven resources are now available to help churches improve their effectiveness. Seminar formats / schedules are individually designed to fit each church's needs.

The most popular seminars are:

- Discover Your Giftedness (UY) church wide seminar and optional certification training.
- Specialist Certification Training (Seminars focusing on specific areas).
- Advanced and NEW Executive Certification Training / Masters Institute & Extreme Personality Makeover Training (for professional trainers & consultants).
- Global Focus Leadership Seminar which features the Uniquely You Profile (See page 128)

Uniquely You also specializes in training trainers, consultants, and personal coaches to be more effective. We offer several training opportunities; such as, Church Assimilation, Discovery Series, Leadership Training, Wellness Dynamics, Human Relations, and Human Behavior Science. Each training is designed to focus on popular personal and corporate development needs. You Do not have to be a natural public speaker or presenter. There are opportunities available to fit your personality / training style.

You may want to just learn how to conduct training using Human Behavior Science resources; such as, our Uniquely You and Discovery Series Profiles. Or you may want to learn how to become one of our presenters and conduct training in churches and/or businesses. We can help you decide how to set up your own ministry/business.

We are especially excited about our new Masters Institute, Extreme Personality Makeover Training / Coaching and Consulting. These seminars are usually conducted through all day or evening Conference Calls. They are recommended for those who have already attended our Basic, Specialist, and Advanced Certification Training and want to go to the next level of competency and credentialing.

Once you complete the MI and / or EPM Training you will have exclusive rights to market and train or coach others with discounted MI and EPM resources, plus the highest level for substantial discounts for all other resources. You will also become a UY Affiliate and receive commissions from the sale of UY online profiles.

Uniquely You focuses on helping others succeed with their people effectiveness needs. Whether it's conducting training, personal consulting, providing resources, or just improving your own personal development, Uniquely You can help you!

Uniquely You now has numerous Profiles, Facilitator Manuals, PowerPoint Presentations and other resources to help you. For example:

Bases Covered Plan Profiles

Discover Membership and Ministry Combination Profiles

Our most popular profiles are the Bases Covered Plan Profiles to help get members involved in ministry. There are four different (7, 9, 16 and 23 spiritual gifts) lists Member's Guides.

Features:
- Uniquely You Questionnaire
- Instructions to complete profile
- Interpretation of DISC Personality Types • Discovering Your Behavioral Blends
- Controlling Your Behavioral Blends • 7, 9, 16, or 23 Spiritual Gifts Questionnaire • Spiritual Gifts Descriptions • Combining Personalities with Spiritual Gifts
- How To Handle Conflicts
- Biblical Resolution Management • Involvement / Personality & Spiritual Gifts Perspective • Fitly Joined Together For Ministry
- Choose You This Day
- Opportunities For Ministry
- Leadership Insights

LEADERSHIP PROFILE

This DISC profile is specifically designed to help professionals and leaders improve their effectiveness by discovering and developing the leader within.

RELATIONSHIP PROFILE

Improve Your Marriage & Pre-marital Counseling, plus Conflict Resolution Challenges with the *UY Relationships Profile* and Small Group Facilitator's Manual. Includes 2 DISC Questionnaires.

Ideal for:
- Personal Development
- Staff Training
- Communications Skills
- Leadership Training
- Coaching & Consulting

Most Profiles can also be completed online.

Go to:
www.UniquelyYou.com
or phone:
(706) 492-5490 for more info.

STARTERS KITS ALSO AVAILABLE

The best and wisest way to get started with any new training program is to first try it with the least investment necessary. Uniquely You has designed many discounted *Starter Kits* so you can investigate and see first-hand how effective our resources are.

Three Ways Uniquely You Human Resources Can Help You!

Over 1,000,000 profiles now in print!

1. Uniquely You Online Certification Training
Become a Certified Trainer or Coach for groups, businesses, and/or schools!

Learn How To Increase Involvement & Reduce Conflicts from the convenience of your phone and computer!

- Certified Church Health Diagnostic Spec. (CHDS)
- Certified Leadership Training Specialist (CLTS)
- Certified Wellness Dynamics Specialist (CWDS)
- Certified Human Relations Specialist (CHRS)
- Certified Human Behavior Consultant (CHBC)
- Certified Church Assimilation Specialist (CCAS)

1 or 2 Day Onsite and / or Conference Call Certification Training —
Basic, Specialist, Advanced, and Executive Training now available.

2. Sponsor a Discover Your Giftedness Seminar and receive FREE Certification Training

Help your members get involved in the activites and responsibilies of your group by identifying their giftedness. Uniquely You now comes on a Love Offering basis, plus a small travel, lodging, and materials fee.

Oak Cliff Bible Fellowship
Uniquely You Seminar — Discover Your Giftedness

Presenters: Dr. Mels Carbonell, Dr. Stan Ponz, or one of their Certified Trainers

Rick Warren, Pastor
Saddleback Church
"One of the best seminars ever!"

Zig Ziglar, Author
"Dr. Mels Carbonell has a message America needs to hear!"

Dr. Tony Evans, Pastor

3. Masters Institute Coaching Conference Calls

Receive personal coaching and consulting on various leadership, team building, health, and professional issues that will make a difference. This 8 weeks (1 1/2 hour sessions) conference call course will use Dr. Carbonell's newest textbooks, *So, you're unique! What's your point?* and *Extreme Personality Makeover* as the text book, along with PowerPoint presentations and Action Plans. Once you complete this course you will be Certified as an Executive Trainer and Affiliate, the highest training and best discounts on resources offered.

MASTERS INSTITUTE

Two courses now available:

"So, You're Unique! What's Your Point?"

"Extreme Personality Makeover!"

Life-Planner Notebook

PowerPoint Presentations

Hardback Books

Life-Planner Notebook

Designed for professional trainers, coaches, consultants, and individuals who want to improve their effectiveness!

You may participate in either or both courses and receive the training without any prerequisites, but if your want to be "certified" and licensed to conduct exclusive training, you must first complete the UY Basic, Specialist, and Advanced Training either at an Onsite or Conference Call Seminar.

Once you complete all four levels of training, you will be a ***Certified Executive Trainer*** eligible for the best discounts.

MI Conference Calls are 8 weeks of 1.5 hours per class.
For more info, go to: www.myuy.com, then click on "Training

www.UniquelyYou.NET

24/7 OnLine
Your Online Profile Store

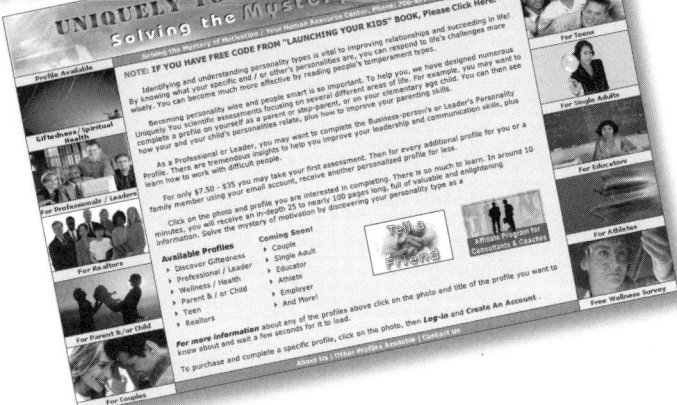

Numerous Online Profiles Available
- Extreme Personality Makeover (faith-based)
- Discover Your Giftedness
  (faith-based with your choice of combining
  4 Spiritual Gifts lists with DISC personality types
- Professionals / Leaders DISC Personalities
  (nearly 100 pages / standard version)
- Realtors DISC Personalities (standard version)
- Parents, Child's, and Teen's DISC Personalities
  (faith-based and standard versions)
- Couples (faith-based or standard versions)

Coming Soon!
- Employers
- Single Adults
- Educators
- Athletes
- And More!

Affiliate Programs
Receive Discounts or Earn Commissions!

Receive discounts or commissions by placing our online profile link on your web site or organization's site. This is a great opportunity for businesses, churches and organizations to offer their members or customers any of our profiles online 24/7, to complete in the convenience of their own homes or offices.

***Become a Partner and
receive substantial discounts!***

For example, if you as an organization, church, business owner or leader want your members, staff, or customers to complete one of our profiles and receive a discount, you can become a Partner.

Simply place our: www.uniquelyyou.NET link on your web Home Page and receive an instant discount for everyone who completes his or her profile through your site.

***Become an Affiliate and
receive unlimited commissions!***

Ground Floor Opportunity!

Uniquely You Profiler

Affiliation Program

If you or your organization becomes one of our Affiliates Masters, you can receive commissions. Basic, Specialist, Advanced, and Executive Certified individuals will continue to receive their discounts for themselves or their organization's phone-in orders.

Affiliates that build a downline with customers who also want to become Affiliates can do so.

***The BEST Commissions and
Consulting Offer Available!***

You can receive commissions for every First Level profile purchased at the current $7.50 or $35 retail price.
(prices tentative / see web page for current prices)

This is a phenomenal offer!

Become a Partner and save, save, save!
Become an Affiliate and earn, earn, earn!

Uniquely You is committed to providing the best human behavioral and biblical resources available, plus helping its consultants and customers improve their effectiveness!

SPONSOR AN
EXTREME PERSONALITY MAKEOVER SEMINAR
FOR YOUR GROUP

If you have never attended one of our Uniquely You seminars, you owe it to yourself to view our web site and take a look at our current seminar schedule (www.myuy.com), or better yet, schedule one of your own!

That's Right! You can host a Uniquely You seminar for your group on a Love Offering basis, plus a small fee for travel, lodging and materials.

Call 1-800-501-0490 for further information.

Oak Cliff Bible Fellowship — Dr. Tony Evans, Pastor

Uniquely You Seminar — Discover Your Giftedness

Uniquely You™ Resources
PO Box 490 • Blue Ridge, GA 30513
e-mail: drmels@myuy.com

*If your company or organization is looking for
results-oriented training for your staff or employees, consider a —*

Improve Your People and Task Skills
Seminar for Professionals and Leaders

Zig Ziglar recommends — *A message America needs to hear!*

Hear why Disney World, DuPont, John Deere, Zig Ziglar,
Acura, AT&T, Southern Bell, Eaton, and Motorola trust
Dr. Mels Carbonell's expertise and training in Human Behavior Science.

What you will learn —

- *THE BIGGEST MISTAKE LEADERS MAKE*
  Managing everyone the same way!

- *SOLVING THE MYSTERY OF MOTIVATION*
  Understanding everyone is motivated!

- *PREDICT RESPONSES / AVOID CONFLICTS*
  Why intimidation and manipulation don't work!

- *HANDLING AND CHANGING POOR ATTITUDES*
  Creating an atmosphere and environment for success!

- *OVERUSING STRENGTHS BECOME ABUSES*
  Guarding the best and avoiding the worst thing about you!

- *CHANGE MANAGEMENT*
  "Reengineering The Corporation" Results!

- *TEAM BUILDING*
  Understanding Why The Biggest Problem In
  Business Is Not Technical — It's Relational!

- *SELLING AND SERVICING*
  How "People Based" Selling and Servicing Works!

Other Onsite or Conference Call Seminars or Training
are offered for: Leaders, Educators, Ministers, Counselors, and
Coaches. For more information, go to: ***www.myuy.com***
and click on: "**Training**" or phone: (800) 501-0490.

INTRODUCING HELPING YOU GROW A GREAT COMMISSION CHURCH

Our passion is to see the global church spiritually revitalized and strategically mobilized to fulfill its role in God's global mission.

The Global Opportunity

These are exciting days in the history of the Church of Jesus Christ. All over the world, God's Spirit is moving to reach a people for His name from every tribe, language and nation. From every corner of the globe, record numbers of new worshippers are being brought into the Kingdom of God.

As leaders, we must empower the local church with creative, contemporary, cutting-edge strategies that will energize God's people to fulfill God's desire for them individually, and the local church corporately.
Dr. Larry Reesor, President
& Founder Global Focus

As the Holy Spirit moves and works, individual Christians and local churches worldwide are embracing their responsibility and awakening to the opportunity they have to be on mission with God. Together they are joining hands to complete the mission He gave the Church.

God has used Global Focus to greatly impact our church. Ninety-three members have committed to long-term missions service and over 2900 have gone on short-term mission trips since 1991. We increased our annual missions giving from $140,000 in 1991 to over $2.5 million in 2001. At the same time our church has greatly expanded its local outreach.
Dr. Johnny Hunt, Pastor Woodstock, GA

The partnership of Global Focus with the International Mission Board and the North American Mission Board has resulted in an unprecedented thrust of mobilization among Southern Baptist Churches.
Dr. Jerry Rankin, President
International Mission Board

One of the most helpful benefits in effectively being On Mission in your daily life is to realize how you are "wired" in your personality, and then learn how to maximize that to help others discover Christ's plan and calling for their lives. We're glad to be working with Uniquely You and the International Mission Board through Global Focus to unleash a movement of Christ-followers who are On Mission to change their world.
Dr. Bob Reccord, President
North American Mission Board

Attend a GF Leadership Seminar and receive FREE Uniquely You Certification!
One of the greatest challenges pastors face is building a cohesive leadership team that identifies with a common, church-wide vision. This is why the Global Focus Leadership Seminar is designed to unite your leaders through a shared biblical vision and a dynamic corporate strategy that will empower you for a more effective local and global impact.

For more info, go to: www.globalfocus.info